THE SECOND GREATEST COMMANDMENT

*"Teacher, which is the greatest
commandment in the Law?"
Jesus replied: "'Love the Lord your God with
all your heart and with all your soul and
with all your mind.' This is the first and
greatest commandment. And the second is
like it: 'Love your neighbor as yourself.'
All the Law and the Prophets
hang on these two commandments."*

THE SECOND GREATEST COMMANDMENT

A CALL TO A PERSONAL AND CORPORATE LIFE OF CARING

WILLIAM M. FLETCHER

NAVPRESS

The Navigators is an international, evangelical Christian organization. Jesus Christ gave his followers the Great Commission to go and make disciples (Matthew 28:19). The aim of The Navigators is to help fulfill that commission by multiplying laborers for Christ in every nation.

NavPress is the publishing ministry of The Navigators. NavPress publications are tools to help Christians grow. Although publications alone cannot make disciples or change lives, they can help believers learn biblical discipleship and apply what they learn to their lives and ministries.

©1983 by William M. Fletcher
All rights reserved, including translation
ISBN: 0-89109-502-0
Library of Congress Catalog Card Number:
83-062501
15024

Unless otherwise identified, Scripture quotations are from *The New American Standard Bible,* ©1960, 1973 by the Lockman Foundation. Other versions used include *Holy Bible: The New International Version,* ©1978 by the New York International Bible Society, used by permission of Zondervan Bible Publishers; and *The Living Bible,* ©1971 by Tyndale House Publishers.

Printed in the United States of America

*To
Jeanette, whose faithfulness
and caring
have been a constant stimulus
to my ministry.*

Contents

About the Author

Dr. William M. Fletcher is pastor of First Baptist Church in Golden, Colorado. He has also served as pastor of Grace Bible Chapel, in Grand Rapids, Minnesota. Previous to his pastoral experience, he spent many years on the Navigator staff, serving in a variety of ministry capacities in the U.S. and Europe, and at International Headquarters in Colorado Springs. For many years he has been active in developing literature for use in personal Bible study, curriculum, and discipling ministries. Dr. Fletcher is a member of the Board of Trustees of the Conservative Baptist Theological Seminary in Denver, Colorado, from which he holds the degree, Doctor of Ministry. He currently serves as Vice President of the Rocky Mountain Conservative Baptist Association. He and his wife, Jeanette, live in Golden, Colorado.

Foreword

This book is by a pastor, but the chapters are far from reshaped sermons. They are products of extensive reading, pastoral visitation, and a systematic plan for training laymen in the overwhelming task of caring for hurting people on our interpersonal battlefields.

I have watched this book as well as its author grow through a Doctor of Ministry program at our seminary. I am happy with the results in both. Books by professors are usually long on theory but short on practice. Books by pastors tend to be high on experiences but low on reasons. Not only has William Fletcher sampled the literature, he has reduced the theories to a workable plan for enlisting laymen in a fundamental responsibility of the church—"the care of souls," as our fathers in the faith once called it.

I have had the pleasure of having Dr. Fletcher's son and his son-in-law in my classes. Both are letters of commendation for a man who practices what he preaches in this book. I share his concern to see the *people* of God undertake the *work* of God in ways that will make a difference in our world. To that end I am happy to join him in sending forth his book with a prayer that more troubled people will find in Jesus Christ the way to hope and healing.

BRUCE L. SHELLEY

Preface

Whatever our view of the Great Commission, we cannot escape the fact that we are commanded to carry the gospel to *people.* We are responsible before God to evangelize and to disciple *people.* Therefore, in order to be successful in accomplishing our mission, we must learn what it is that people most respond to.

¶ I am one of those fairly well organized types. I can administer activities and affairs until the machinery of the church runs rather smoothly. I can teach the Scriptures quite logically (at least so I think). There came a time in my pastoral ministry, however, when I realized that I had been expecting to be successful with these qualities alone. Much to my dismay, people were not responding as I had hoped to my flawless organization and impeccable logic.

As this realization dawned on me, it seemed that the Lord was telling me that I had missed an important point in the ministry. The entities I was dealing with were *people,* not machines! And people respond to love. As I analyzed my life and ministry I found that I needed to grow in love—*agape* love. Then as I surveyed the church I was serving, I found, as one might expect, a reflection of myself. The church needed to grow in love. As the Deacons and I discussed this we decided that we had to adjust our thinking. We would strive to make our church a caring church.

As we studied our situation more carefully, we saw that many needs were going unmet. Perhaps each of us was too busy with his part in the church program. If we had only stopped to pay attention, we would surely have noticed that people around us were suffering. We began to see that, regardless of excuses, we were not loving as we ought to. Body life was not a functioning reality. Our fellowship didn't go deep enough. Our hearts were not sensitive enough.

As a result of this self-study, we began to take some definite steps to meet some of the needs we saw. This action led to what we at first called "a caring model."

¶ Our revolution at First Baptist Church in Golden, Colorado began when I preached a "state of the church" message on Sunday morning, January 8, 1978. I challenged our people to get involved in the growth of our church. Over one hundred people volunteered that day to help build our fellowship. One of the options I offered them was to be available to care for others in need. A number of people said they wanted to give themselves to such a ministry.

To prepare these people for such a caring ministry, we set up a thirteen-week training program, which was taught as an adult elective during one Sunday school quarter. This book evolved out of that training curriculum. My hope is that it might serve as a training manual for other caring groups. Our experience has shown that people want to be trained. Most of those who have been in these classes (which we offer each year) have said they had wanted to help others but felt inadequate. We have taught them biblical principles for caring as well as practical skills needed for such a ministry.

When we began this caring program, we prayed that it would bring some lasting results in the church. Our goals were: 1) that a few people would come to a conceptual understanding of what New Testament caring is, as well as learning some basic skills; 2) that the needs of more people might be met, which would otherwise be overlooked; and 3) that such caring people would grow in numbers and in influence, stimulating the entire church family to begin to grow as a healing community. We are realizing these goals. The Deacons have observed an increasing depth in the spiritual life of our church. People are beginning to respond spontaneously to needs around them. More money has come into the Deacons Fund (used to assist people with special needs). Visitors are more often commenting that this is a caring church. Some other caring ministries have sprung up as a result of our initial program.

¶ I've shared more details about our ministry venture throughout this book, and the appendix outlines a suggested program for implementing a caring ministry in the local church. My prayer is that we all might grow in our ability to "Bear one another's burdens, and thus fulfill the law of Christ" (Galatians 6:2).

PART ONE

Caring Because Jesus Cared

1
Does Anybody Really Care?

I've rejoined the human race!" This is the enthusiastic testimony of a man whose life had been changed by the caring ministry of several men in our church. This man had scraped bottom. He had been ready to quit. Then four of our men stepped in to offer help—not just advice, but genuine help that cost them time, effort, and money. This is caring!

Many people in our local churches are hurting deep inside their smiling exteriors. They can point to a born-again experience in their lives. We see them in the pew every Sunday. We discover in casual conversation that they know their Bible. In fact, they probably know all the pat answers to the problems of life—yet for some reason it hasn't helped. Many are like Charles Schultz's cartoon character Linus, who plucked petals from a daisy while reciting, "Does anybody up there (out there . . . down there) care?"

These people are looking for assurance that someone cares. They may wonder about the rest of the congregation "out there." Sure, the others are usually pleasant at the Sunday morning service, but do they really care about their fellow worshipers the rest of the week? When people "out there" don't seem to care, there tend to be doubts about "up there" too.

Does God really care? If asked that question, most of these sufferers would respond positively. They would not deny the Scriptures: God says he cares. Somehow, though, many find it difficult to see how such promises touch the real world where they live. These strugglers in life may even be able to quote such helpful verses as 1 Peter 5:7—"casting all your anxiety upon Him, because He cares for you." Yet they may still be suffering in loneliness, or sinking deeper into despair over the loss of a loved one. They don't seem to be able to translate the promises of Scripture into meaningful support in times of distress.

Some hurting people are like the little girl who awoke in terror several times during the night from a recurring nightmare. Her mother hurried to her side each time to comfort and reassure her. Each time she quietly shared Bible verses with the child and prayed with her, yet the little girl's fear persisted. She just didn't want her mother to leave her side. Finally, in desperation, the mother said, "But honey, Jesus is with you."

"Yes I know," the child answered, tears streaming down her face, "but I need someone with skin on!"

This is the cry of many a hurting person: a longing for "someone with skin on"—a fellow human who cares and is there.

¶ The ultimate act of love has, of course, already been performed. Even a casual reading of the New Testament brings us face to face with the love of God expressed in and through

Jesus Christ. God the Father demonstrated his love for us by sending heaven's best, his Son, to die for our sins (John 3:16). This divine example shows us God's selfless motivation, generous giving, and intimate involvement with people, the objects of his love. Further, notice in Romans 5:8 that God gave his love to us even though it is not deserved, and regardless of our response: "But God demonstrates His own love toward us, in that while we were yet sinners, Christ died for us." This is unquestionably the highest level of love. The New Testament uses the Greek word, *agape* to set this kind of love apart from all forms of human love. Jeremiah gave it one of its finest expressions in the Old Testament: "I have loved you with an everlasting love; therefore I have drawn you with loving kindness" (Jeremiah 31:3).

This love is fully explained in the New Testament. The sin which stands between God and man, the barrier which makes us unworthy of God's love, has been taken away by Jesus' death on the cross. The greatness of His love is magnified when we realize that the innocent died to pay for the sins of the guilty. Jesus Christ, the sinless one, died for us. Our Savior is the crowning revelation of the love of God. This love has not only been declared in words in the Scriptures, it has been declared in a life. Jesus Christ is the unmistakable expression of the love of God. A careful look at the Savior should dispel our fear of being unloved.

The life of Jesus, clearly presented in the gospels, is a life of love. As Benjamin Warfield observed,

> In the synoptic portrait of Christ the trait which stands out most clearly is the love of Jesus. He not only commanded love, but first Himself practiced it. It is not merely His thought but His will, and not merely His will but above all His deed.[1]

If love is real, it will be expressed. If it is God's love *(agape),* it will be expressed sacrificially. Divine love cannot remain silent or uninvolved! People are waiting for its expression—for someone to get involved with them where they live and work. They have heard of the love of Jesus as it is taught in the Scriptures and preached from our pulpits. They are looking, however, for the living example.

Many of us have the "of course I love you" attitude. We're like the man who, when his wife asked if he loved her, responded matter-of-factly, "I told you I loved you when we were married, and that if there were any change I'd let you know." Relationships do not survive on such attitudes. Rather, good relationships are built upon the voluntary expression of divine love.

People around us are waiting for us to tell them we care and then act as if we mean it. Jesus not only had a mind to love, he practiced it. He left no doubt in the minds of those he rubbed shoulders with. They knew he cared, because his caring touched their lives and made a difference. In the same way, greeting on the church steps is simply not enough. It may be a good beginning, but it often leaves a persistent emptiness unrelieved by the momentary pleasantry. A suffering person may go his way still wondering if he could ever confide in or rely on the greeter. Uncertain, he may plod home, wondering whether *anybody* really cares.

Left untended, this kind of situation can steadily worsen. One young man complained bitterly to me, "I wasn't making it financially. My business was failing. No one cared." He and his family had attended church regularly. Friends had chatted with them freely. He and his wife had been invited into the homes of other young couples. Despite these expressions of interest, however, no one had learned of his deep concerns. He had seen other people receiving help but had not been able to bring himself to confess his pressing needs, and so the burden had persisted and grown heavier. No one had seemed to recognize he was crying for help, so he had left the church. When this became known the church leaders were nagged by questions of guilt. Was it our fault? Did we really show love? Did we listen? Did we give him the freedom to unburden his concerns? Have others left our church because they felt we didn't care?

This unfortunate occurrence happens in our churches more often than we'd like to admit. When it does we may try to justify ourselves by rationalizing: *We're sure we showed enough love. He should have told us about his complaints.* But we have to admit that no one really got intimately involved. No one got close enough to listen. If love had been expressed in a way that made him feel free to open up, perhaps it would have turned out differently.

Of course, this is only one instance. Every pastor can offer similar examples from his experience—for example, the young single or divorcee who always feels left out in a society geared for couples. Or the person who lives with some shame or embarrassment from his past and never feels accepted. Perhaps it is the recently widowed lady whose pillow is wet with tears shed in agony over her loss. Many have commented, "How well she is doing!" "How good she looks!" But no one calls, and she struggles through long evenings and long holidays alone!

Where are those who will care? Where are those who will express the love of God to these heartsick and lonely people, quietly accepting them and helping them practically in whatever way they need?

¶ It has been said that "God always behaves like himself." How grateful we should be that this is so. We learn that "God is love." But it is important to remember that God, who dwells in every born-again believer, is *always* love, and he wants to express his love through us. Paul tells us in Galatians that the fruit of the Spirit is love. If we truly are Spirit-indwelt, we should be showing that love. The Holy Spirit does not express hate, nor envy, nor a careless, self-centered, unconcerned attitude toward others. These are products of the sinful nature, the flesh. Where the Spirit is in control there is love. Such love will demand expression.

Love naturally flows from our lives because we share the nature of God. Warren Wiersbe has described this nature in us as though it were a compass:

> A navigator depends on a compass to help him determine his course. But why a compass? Because it shows him his directions. And why does the compass point north? Because it is so constituted that it responds to the magnetic field of the earth.[2]

The Christian is made to be responsive to the nature of God. His life should show that his response to God's nature is as reliable as the response of the compass to the magnetic field. All who come near him should sense the presence and love of God. In a very real sense, his life should point the people he rubs shoulders with to God. They should begin to see God's love through him.

This directing effect that the Christian has on others is illustrated by the story of the man who was hurrying through an airport terminal, late for his flight. In his haste he overlooked a little girl in front of him, who was carrying a jigsaw puzzle in a box. When he collided with her the puzzle pieces were scattered helter-skelter across the floor. Instead of rushing on, as he was no doubt tempted to do, he stopped and helped the youngster pick up the pieces. When the entire puzzle was back in its box, the little girl looked up at him and said, "Mister, you must have missed your plane." The man smiled and answered, "So I have." Then the girl asked in all sincerity, "Mister, are you Jesus?"

Such is the life of a person who cares and is willing to stop and get involved. It costs something, but it produces something worthwhile. And that is so gratifying that the cost seems to fade into insignificance. When we stop to care we often discover that we can be used of God in simple but effective ways. It doesn't take great skill, just a loving, giving heart and a willingness to take the time. In giving ourselves to others, we find ourselves. When we acknowledge the worth of another, we discover our own worth!

¶ When we started a caring program in our church many people were interested, but some felt they were not qualified. This apprehension is understandable. We place so much emphasis on talent or an attractive personality that average Christians feel they aren't needed. Caring, however, is something every Christian can do. The chief qualification is willingness—first to let God have control of our life, and then to let him express his love through us.

Probably no one in Jesus' day seemed less qualified for this ministry than the sons of Zebedee, James and John. These tough fishermen were known as the "sons of thunder." On one occasion, when a group of Samaritans turned them away, they said to Jesus, "Lord, do You want us to command fire to come down from heaven and consume them?" (Luke 9:54). This is hardly a caring response. As they walked with Jesus, however, he transformed their lives. They became sensitive, caring men. John became known as the apostle of love.

Our loving God can perform this miracle for each of us. We can become caring persons who delight to get involved in helping others. We saw a beautiful example of this in the first stages of our church caring program. A need came to my attention in the life of a man who had recently lost his wife (let's call him Don). In addition to his loneliness, Don was suffering from a heart condition as well as another debilitating disease. As if this were not enough for one man to bear, he was also in serious financial need, and his car was about to be repossessed. At this point in his life it seemed to Don that no one cared about him. He felt there was no way out and even attempted suicide. Then the tide turned when some of the men of our church heard of his plight. One man in particular spent time with him listening, encouraging, and praying with him. Then several men who cared helped him get on his feet financially. They helped him sell his car and buy one within his means. One of the men, a mechanic, put this car in good working order for him without charging for his labor. Another man continued to keep in touch with Don on a daily basis for a while, then met with him weekly for a period of time.

As a result Don began to testify of the goodness of God. He told his friends around the community how his Christian brothers had helped him in a time of need. His countenance changed, and his health seemed to improve. He began to read his Bible again and to join enthusiastically in our church fellowship. He had rejoined the human race.

Would you like to be used to care for a brother or a sister who is down? God can use you if you are willing.

On Your Own

1. Look up John 3:16 and Romans 5:8. How has God demonstrated his love for us? *By sending Christ Jesus to die for us.*

2. "God always behaves like himself." In your own words, write out Jeremiah 31:3 and 1 Peter 5:7, and then answer this question: How do you know that God continues to care for you? *Because Gods love is everlasting.*

3. As a first step in caring for others, make a list of three people who you know are hurting. Write down a specific request for each person, and pray for them each day this week.

Aunt Lillie - Physical pain.
Mildred - Emotional / Family Pain
Mary Haire - " " "

2
Starting with Love

W hat is REAL?' asked the Rabbit one day before Nana came to tidy the room. 'Does it mean having things that buzz inside you and a stick-out handle?'

"'Real isn't how you are made,' said the Skin Horse. 'It's a thing that happens to you. When a child loves you for a long, long time, not just to play with, but REALLY loves you, then you become Real.'

"'Does it hurt?' asked the Rabbit.

"'Sometimes,' said the Skin Horse, for he was always truthful. 'When you are real you don't mind being hurt.'

"'Does it happen all at once, like being wound up,' he asked, 'or bit by bit?'

"'It doesn't happen all at once,' said the Skin Horse. 'You become. It takes a long time. That's why it doesn't often happen to people who break easily, or have sharp edges, or who have to be carefully kept. Generally, by the time you are Real, most of your hair has been loved off, and your eyes drop out and you get loose in the joints and very shabby. But these things don't matter at all, because once you are Real you can't be ugly, except to the people who don't understand.'"[1]

Remarkable changes usually do take place in people when they realize they are loved. It is then they often find their place in life, or, as children's author Margery Williams has described it, they become "real." And who of us doesn't want to become real? We all want to be loved, to be needed, to be cared for. However, to turn that around and care for another with the same commitment isn't so easy.

"People are unreasonable, illogical, and self-centered. Love them anyway!" This sentiment from a popular poster is admirable for its good intent, but how do we do it? Where do we find the resources to love the unlovely? Certainly, if we are empty vessels that are starved for such love ourselves, we have nothing to give to others.

¶ Some might suggest that we must love others because it is our duty to love. But the way of duty is not always enough to keep us motivated.

In his poem entitled "The Second Mile," Stephen Moore suggests that duty often gives way to love:

Stern Duty said, "Go walk a mile
    And help thy brother bear his load."
I walked reluctant, but meanwhile,
    My heart grew soft with help bestowed.
Then Love said, "Go another mile."
    I went, and Duty spoke no more,
But Love arose and with a smile
    Took all the burden that I bore.
'Tis ever thus when duty calls;
    If we spring quickly to obey,

Love comes, and whatsoe'er befalls,
   We're glad to help another day.
The second mile we walk with joy;
   Heaven's peace goes with us in the road,
So let us all our powers employ
   To help our brother bear life's load.

Moore's observation that we often begin to care only because we feel obligated is a valid one. He is also correct in noting that once we begin to express such care, love often takes over, motivating us, strengthening us, and enabling us to give of ourselves even when we are weary in well-doing. However, our question remains unanswered. What do we do if we just don't seem to have any love? No matter how strong the pressure of duty, it cannot draw love from a dry well. We would probably all agree that such a resource of love *should* exist within the heart of every believer, and that it should well up and overflow when a need arises. In all honesty, however, most of us must admit that this is not always so.

Why do believers have trouble loving others? Was there something missing in our conversion? That is one possiblity—certainly there are pretenders in the ranks of every Christian assembly. But assuming that we are among the redeemed, that we have the assurance of an eternal relationship with God, we have to look harder for an explanation of why we often do not find it within us to reach out to another in need.

Perhaps Charles Schultz's cartoon character Linus provides us with a clue. Big sister Lucy is making fun of him:

Lucy—You a doctor! Ha! That's a big laugh! You could never be a doctor! You know why? Because you don't love mankind, that's why!

Linus (finally aroused, he shouts back)—I love mankind . . . it's people I can't stand!

Strange as it may seem, Linus speaks for many a professing Christian. It isn't that we hate people in general; we are not misanthropists. It's just that we have difficulty showing love to *individuals*—it's too costly. The demands of love are too great. It's threatening. We don't feel safe giving ourselves to others. It's . . . well, sometimes it's just impossible.

¶ Author John Powell once asked a friend of his who was a psychiatrist, "How can you teach people to love?" In his answer the learned doctor pointed out that we are like someone with a toothache, totally occupied with our own suffering: "This is a pain-filled world in which we are living. And the pains that reside deep in the human hearts around us are not unlike toothaches. We go to bed with them at night and we wake up with them in the morning. . . . Most human beings are so turned-in by their own pains that they cannot get enough out of themselves to love to any great extent."[2]

Somehow, then, we must be making progress in overcoming our own problems before we can reach out in love to others. Jesus seemed to be aware of this when he answered the lawyer's question in Matthew 22. The lawyer, an expert in the Mosaic law, had asked him, "Teacher, which is the great commandment in the Law?" Jesus' answer was both definitive and authoritative:

> And He said to him, "'You shall love the Lord your God
> with all your heart, and with all your soul, and with
> all your mind.' This is the great and foremost
> commandment. And the second is like it, 'You shall love
> your neighbor as yourself.' On these two commandments
> depend the whole Law and the Prophets."

Jesus summarized the keeping of the Ten Commandments in terms of love. He spoke of Godward love first, then of manward love. These statements, he said, summarize all of the Ten Commandments and all that the prophets taught. The first command deals with our walk with God, the second with our behavior among men. It is no accident that his answer is given in this order: first, God did give the commandments in this order (see Exodus 20). Second, this is the order in which we must obey them. When the vertical relationship is right, our relationships on the horizontal plane are apt to be right. When our experience of God's love is daily, soul-inspiring and life-changing, then our capacity to love others will also be growing. Then we'll begin to find we are compelled to reach out.

¶ Maurice E. Wagner, a professional counselor, says that Jesus gives us a healthy foundation for personhood and a healthy prescription for caring in his answer to the lawyer. Wagner observes, "Obeying the first great commandment redeems us from the bondage of self-verification."[3] This obedience sets us free as objects of God's love, Wagner declares, releasing us to love others selflessly:

> . . . we are free to enjoy others for what they really are. . . . Having discovered that we are somebody to God, we automatically regard others as somebody also. Instead of loving others because we need to be loved by them, we find ourselves loving others because we are loved by God, and most of all, we feel loving. . . . So we no longer maneuver to prove ourselves to others . . . to gain status . . . or to avoid criticism. . . . We gladly affirm others, but we do not play the game of transactional self-verification, trading love for love or hate for hate.[4]

It may be that "automatically" loving others slightly over-states the case, yet it is clear that a secure position in God's love does provide the potential and the basis for loving our brothers in a wholesome way.

A young woman who was a convert from a certain sect illustrates what it means to be set free to love. Since she was also recently divorced, one would have expected Jill (not her real name) to be cautious of giving love, especially if there seemed to be any risk involved. However, the transformation she experienced when Christ came into her life seemed to liberate her completely. Just a short time after her conversion she learned that a friend from her hometown, accused of killing her husband during a quarrel, was in jail awaiting trial for murder. As soon as Jill learned of her friend's plight she began to pray for her and then called her long-distance to offer her support and friendship. The accused woman began to respond, so Jill took time off work to be with her during the trial. Thus Jill was able not only to share her verbal witness but also to extend an unusual display of love. This was a convincing testimony of the reality of God's love to one in deep trouble.

Jill's case shows us how important it is that we experience God's love first; neighbor-love will follow. Such experience of divine love has its beginning in our conversion and grows as we live in fellowship with God. It is a byproduct of a healthy daily devotional practice of feeding upon God's word and communicating with him in prayer. This daily practice will condition us and motivate us to express love to those around us.

¶ When Jesus answered the lawyer's question in Matthew 22, he revealed his awareness of the importance of self-love: "You shall love your neighbor as yourself." The apostle Paul also recognized this same human characteristic in his injunction to husbands: "So husbands ought also to love their own wives as their own bodies. He who loves his own wife loves himself" (Ephesians 5:28). Are these passages speaking of sinful pride or of healthy self-esteem? This has long been a nagging question in Bible-believing circles. We have been taught that self-love is at the root of our sin problem which separates us from God. This teaching is certainly good theology. It points to the kind of inordinate self-love expressed in the words of Lucifer himself:

But you said in your heart, "I will ascend to heaven;
I will raise my throne above the stars of God. . . .
I will make myself like the Most High." (Isaiah 14:13-14)
Similar words are also attributed by Ezekiel to the prince of
Tyre, and God warns him,

Because your heart is lifted up and you have said,
"I am a god, I sit in the seat of gods,
In the heart of the seas"; Yet you are a man
and not God. . . . (Ezekiel 28:2)

It is inordinate self-love when a human being exalts himself
to the position of deity. This kind of self-love usually has two
manifestations, both of which are sin: first, a man claims the
right to run his own life and to go his own way without God,
and second, he places himself over others. The "I am better
than you" philosophy is usually a product of the first mani-
festation. In either case, a mere man is playing god. This is a
sinful self-love rather than a healthy self-acceptance.

In this sinful condition, we cannot express a healthy love
for another, whether spouse or neighbor. An excessive self-
love sets up barriers between ourselves and our fellow man.
For these reasons, Paul warns every believer "not to think
more highly of himself than he ought to think" (Romans 12:3).
And he further urges the Philippian believers, "Do nothing
from selfishness or empty conceit, but with humility of mind
let each of you regard one another as more important than
himself" (Philippians 2:3).

¶ Does the command to love our neighbor as ourself suggest
a healthy self-esteem? Yes, for this kind of self-esteem is to be
found in a right relationship to God, which sets us free to love
others. Self-centeredness says, "I'm the one who is important.
In fact, I am more important than my neighbor." Healthy
self-esteem says, "I'm important because God says I'm important to him." The healthy Christian is able to make a sensible

appraisal of himself before God. He does not think of himself more highly than he ought but is able to make a sound judgment of his position of acceptance before God. He is then also able to make a generous assessment of his neighbor.

As we begin to understand what God thinks of us, we'll learn to think of ourselves in the same way. When we think meanly of ourselves, however, we are ignoring the position of favor God has given to us. We become insecure and fearful, afraid to reach out, and thus apt to withdraw from people. We can easily sink to such a low level of self-esteem that we'll find ourselves waiting for others to help us; we have no strength to offer them. We are then possessed by a negative brand of self-love, which sees only our own needs.

This focus on self happens because we have failed to accept our positive position of favor in the eyes of our caring heavenly Father. As a result, we tend to see everything, and everybody, as threatening to us. We will find that we are unable to talk about anything but ourselves, and we in fact may become very angry at those who will not pay attention to us. In such a state we are of no use to God or man, and we may become so depressed that we have no use for ourselves.

What a deplorable condition for a child of the King! When we find ourselves in this downward spiral it is time to review the greatness of God's love for us. We can turn to passages such as Jeremiah 31:3, in which the prophet quotes God as he expresses his love for his people: "I have loved you with an everlasting love; Therefore I have drawn you with loving-kindness." God's love is unceasing; it never fails. Isaiah spoke of a time when Israel bemoaned, "The Lord has forsaken me, And the Lord has forgotten me" (Isaiah 49:14). But God's answer came quickly from the prophet's pen: "Can a woman forget her nursing child, And have no compassion on the son of her womb? Even these may forget, but I will not forget you" (verse 15).

We must be careful not to ascribe our human weaknesses to God, and instead lift our hearts to him in thanksgiving for his unceasing love. We should also remind our weary hearts that God loved us even though we were in a state of rebellion: "But God demonstrates His own love toward us, in that while we were yet sinners, Christ died for us" (Romans 5:8). He initiated love for us; we did not approach him. John declares it clearly: "In this is love, not that we loved God, but that He loved us and sent His Son to be the propitiation for our sins" (1 John 4:10). Self-esteem begins to build as we realize that the great God of eternity has such an overwhelming love for us. It is in the wake of such a realization that our hearts can burst into song, joining the hymn writer who wrote,

Loved with everlasting love,
    Led by grace that love to know,
Spirit breathing from above,
    Thou hast taught me it is so.
Oh, this full and perfect peace!
    Oh, this transport all divine!
In a love which cannot cease,
    I am His and He is mine.

Basking in such love, we can no longer think of ourselves as unimportant to God. And lifted by the realization of his great love, we are compelled to love him in return. It is no chore, then, to love the Lord our God with all our heart, all our soul, and all our mind. And from this Godward love there flows quite naturally a love for our neighbor.

A healthy self-esteem, then, is a result of seeing ourselves as God sees us. Realizing that we are held firmly in the arms of his great love, we are secure. Nothing can threaten us; we can now risk loving others. In fact, we'll find we cannot restrain the overflow of the love of God which possesses our hearts. A graduate student shared this testimony of her struggle with self-esteem:

Most of my early years were spent trying to get people to like me—probably because I didn't like myself. I needed to have people depend on me to have a sense of importance. Organizations, choirs, and other groups became my reason for living. I became a teacher and coach—now I can see that this merely legitimized my hunger for having people depend on me.

Not until about three years ago did I realize that my self-image was based on other people. I'd been a Christian about four years at that time. I guess the Lord decided that was the next area he was going to work on, because he removed some of my closest friends (marriage, moves, etc.) and I had to turn to him completely.

Through teaching and fellowship with other Christians, I began to understand that he loves and accepts me as I am. If I accepted myself, I could cooperate in his process of conforming me to Christ's image. If I didn't, I usually fought against that process.

Once I accepted the basic idea of God's love for me, I found that I no longer had the unhealthy attitude of relying on others for my self-worth. I could reach out to them because God loves me and wants me to share that love with them.

No longer do I live in fear that others will reject me—now I can freely share God's unconditional love for me with those to whom he guides me. Of course, this process is not yet complete, but the difference is astounding even now.

Verna Birkey tells us in her book, *You Are Someone Very Special,* "You are deeply loved by Him, a person of value."[5] This is a solid basis for sharing with others. *You* have much to share. Begin now to reach up with thanksgiving and to reach out with love.

On Your Own

1. Pray over Psalm 139:1-18, and write down every indication that you are special to God. Thank him for each item you have listed.

2. Read carefully 1 Peter 1:18-19 and 1 John 3:1-2. What is the cost, and the result, of God's love for you?

3. Telephone or write a note to someone who needs encouragement. Share with him or her one of the truths from Scripture that you have just studied.

1. He knows my laying down and rising up.
He knows my thoughts
He directs my path. He knows my ways.
He knows my mind. He surrounds me.
He is with me always. His hand leads me.
He formed my inward parts.
His thoughts are many and precious to me.

2. It cost Jesus blood. We were made children of God.

3. Write Thelma. Cast her cares upon Jesus, He cares for her.

3
Compassion for the Whole Man

A man lies injured along the dusty road from Jerusalem to Jericho. Another man comes by, riding on a donkey. When he sees the injured man he immediately stops, leans over, and asks in a concerned tone, "Do you have Blue Cross?"

This kind of scenario is repeated in a cartoon by Charles Schulz. Snoopy is shivering in a snowstorm as Linus and Charlie Brown come walking by, snug and warm in their thick winter coats.

> Charlie Brown—"Snoopy looks kind of cold, doesn't he?"
> Linus—"I'll say he does . . . maybe we'd better go over and comfort him."
> Linus to Snoopy—"Be of good cheer, Snoopy."
> Charlie Brown—"Yes, be of good cheer."

They walk away, leaving Snoopy questioning the meaning of the encounter—while he continues to shiver.

The apostle John drives the point home:

> We know love by this, that He laid down His life for
> us; and we ought to lay down our lives for the brethren.
> But whoever has the world's goods, and beholds his
> brother in need and closes his heart against him,
> how does the love of God abide in him? (1 John 3:16-17)

¶ It's been said that compassion is a "Jesus term" in the New Testament. The term most often used *(splagchna)* was the strongest word in the Greek language to describe compassion. The Greeks of New Testament times believed that deep emotions were associated with certain inner organs of the body. The term for compassion denoted the major organs—heart, lungs, liver, even intestines—as the sources of such feelings. (We have a similar expression in English: "I love you with all my heart.") The King James version translates the Greek term as "bowels of compassion," meaning that a person is moved from the very depths of his being to help another.

Writing on the emotional life of Jesus, Benjamin Warfield has said that compassion is the master-motive of our Savior:

> The emotion which we should naturally expect to find
> most frequently attributed to Jesus whose whole life
> was a mission of mercy, and whose ministry was so
> marked by deeds of beneficence that it was summed
> up in the memory of His followers as going through the
> land "doing good" (Acts 10:38), is no doubt compassion.
> In fact, this is the emotion which is most frequently
> attributed to Him. The term employed to express it
> (splagchna) is perhaps a coinage of the Jewish
> dispersion. . . . The divine mercy has been defined as
> that essential perfection in God "whereby He pities and
> relieves the miseries of His creatures:" It includes . . .
> two parts of an internal movement of pity and an
> external movement of beneficence.[1]

Warfield affirms that the only source of true compassion is God. It was on display in rich, attractive tones in the earthly life of Jesus. Such true compassion is not just a feeling, however deep it might be: It is goodness in action prompted by a deep inner concern.

¶ Even a casual reading of the New Testament reveals that Jesus consistently expressed his love in acts of compassion on behalf of needy people. He demonstrated a concern not only for the spiritual well-being of those he ministered to, but also for their physical well-being. As Dean Turner expresses it, "Matchlessly and perfectly, Jesus cared for the fulfillment of every human being's need in life."[2] It is also important to note that Jesus' compassionate involvement with people where they hurt always led to a ministry to their spiritual needs. He did this when he rescued the woman from death who had been caught in the act of adultery. Thus he saved her physically (John 8:3-10). But he also ministered to her spiritually when he said, "Neither do I condemn you; go your way; from now on sin no more" (verse 11). Modern Christians too often attempt to "win souls" while ignoring the obvious physical needs of those they approach. Jesus never separated the two.

The New Testament shows us repeatedly that Jesus was motivated strongly and urgently by a compassion for people in need. For example, as he looked over the crowds that listened to him, "seeing the multitudes, He felt compassion for them, because they were distressed and downcast like sheep without a shepherd" (Matthew 9:36). This same compassion stirred him to action on behalf of suffering humanity. As he ministered to people in the mountains of Galilee, thousands followed him from the towns and villages of the area. He healed many who were crippled, blind, and dumb (Matthew 15:29-31). However, his concern for these people was even more obvious and touched the entire crowd of four thousand when he said, "I feel compassion for the multitude, because they have remained with Me now for three days and have nothing to eat; and I do not wish to send them away hungry, lest they faint on the way" (verse 32). Thus he fed them all by a miraculous provision (verses 33-38).

Jesus' compassion reached out to the whole man. He was concerned with people and their problems, both physical and spiritual.

¶ Jesus taught this same kind of compassion in three of his parables. Each one uses the same Greek term for compassion (*splagchna*), and in each Jesus taught concern for the whole man.

In the first parable, the master who forgave his slave's debt showed compassion (Matthew 18:23-33). This parable was in answer to Peter's question of how often one must forgive his brother—seven times, as had been taught? Jesus gave a direct answer first, declaring that one must keep on forgiving, and then told the story of a poor slave whose debt was far beyond his means. The master threatened to sell all the members of the slave's household to recover his losses. This action would inevitably have split up the family, perhaps forever. The slave's impassioned appeal moved the master, however, and the master forgave the entire debt.

This story portrays the compassionate forgiveness of God. It also illustrates man's responsibility to demonstrate the same kind of compassion in forgiving his brother: Notice that the forgiven slave refused to forgive those who were indebted to him (verses 28-34). Jesus then made it clear that he is displeased when those who have experienced God's compassionate forgiveness do not in turn show it to their brothers.

Jesus also taught compassion by using the parable of the good Samaritan (Luke 10:29-37). The purpose of this story is to teach what it means to love our neighbor, and particularly to answer the question, "Who is my neighbor?" The religious figures in the story, the priest and the Levite, were unwilling to be inconvenienced (and perhaps unwilling to risk being ceremonially contaminated) by stopping to help the severely beaten man who had been left for dead. They knew the Law as a legalistic system, but they had failed to grasp the spirit of the Law, which required them to be compassionate at any cost (see Matthew 22:37-40). The Samaritan, an outsider to the Jews of that day, was the one who revealed true compassion: He was willing to pay the price to help someone in need. When he saw the wounded man, "he felt compassion." He delayed his journey, took care of the man's needs from his own supplies, and paid for the man's lodging and care with his own money. This kind of behavior is compassionate caring in practice.

The third parable in this group is the story of the prodigal son (Luke 15:11-32). The point of interest for us here is the father's compassion in welcoming home his wayward son—a remarkable illustration of complete forgiveness and restoration to full fellowship. The father illustrates the compassion shown by God in forgiving his repentant children, but his behavior also suggests the pattern for believers to follow. The brother who remained with his father illustrated overwhelming self-centeredness when his prodigal brother returned. He was so occupied with himself and his own rights that he wasn't able to see the beauty of his father's compassion. He completely missed the part such compassion plays in the restoration of a life. This blindness may well describe the condition of many Christians.

In each of these three parables, a turning point occurred when an inner stirring in a person's heart led him to give himself to help another in need. Each of those three people—the forgiving master, the generous Samaritan, and the loving father—cared for another even though that needy person did not seem to deserve such care, or perhaps was not a desirable object of care. This is Jesus' concept of compassion. This is Jesus' concept of caring.

¶ Someone has said, "We have no permission from Jesus to be selective in our compassion." It is our natural tendency, however, to choose whom we will reach out to. Perhaps this was the problem of the priest and the Levite in the parable of the good Samaritan. In any event, we know it is often *our* problem. Jesus mingled with all men, the rich and the poor, the socially acceptable and the backward and undesirable. This willingness to enter into others' lives is costly. A contemporary poet, Michael Quoist, pinpoints our problem:

> Lord, why did you tell me to love all men as my brothers?
> I have tried, but I come back to you frightened.
> Lord, I was so peaceful at home, so comfortably settled.
> It was well-furnished, and I felt so cozy.
> I was alone—I was at peace.
> Sheltered from the wind and the rain, kept clean.

Our God wants to dislodge us from our comfortable, smug existence, to move us to mingle with our needy brothers, to stir us to touch those we might otherwise shun. Another poet, whose name is lost in history, expresses the challenge well: "Love has a hem to her garment that trails in the very dust; it can reach the stains of the streets and lanes, and because it can, it must." This is clearly the brand of compassion Jesus exemplified, and it is the kind of loving outreach he calls us to in our modern world. Answering his call is often a struggle for us. We may pay lip service to such compassion, but the performance is often costly, and we're inclined to back away.

Pastors are no exception to this struggle, myself included. I was reminded of the day several years ago when I received a call asking me to visit an Indian who was being held in the county jail. He had been arrested as an accomplice in an armed robbery. I found myself reacting against this call from the beginning. It was very easy to make excuses—and there was truth in all of them. Yet, despite all my rationalizing, I knew I had to go to call on John.

From the beginning of my first encounter with John, I knew God had led. John seemed to be honest and open. He admitted his mistakes and his need to pay his debt to society. Through our church people, we were able to locate a suit of clothes for him to wear to his trial. Meanwhile, John received Christ into his life, and we gave him a Bible and other literature. He was found guilty as charged and sentenced to three years at the state correctional facility at Buena Vista, Colorado. From his letters and through the prison chaplain we learned that John was reading the Bible, praying, and witnessing to other prisoners.

Thus a little compassion paid off. Even though it was offered reluctantly, God used it to transform a life. It was most gratifying to receive a Christmas card from John, beautifully designed by him. And it was even more rewarding later to receive a note telling of his approaching release, and of his plans to return to his native New Mexico and to witness to his relatives there.

¶ In order to make compassionate caring work, we must be giving a lot but expecting little. A poster I saw in an alcoholic rehabilitation center expressed it well:

I want to . . . love you without clutching, appreciate you without judging, join you without invading, invite you without demanding, leave you without guilt, criticize you without blaming, and help you without insulting.

If I can have the same from you, then we can truly meet and enrich each other.

This goal is idealistic, but it contains the basic principles of a good caring attitude. It means loving a person even though we may despise some of his practices. It involves leading him gently and with respect for his personhood. It is giving with no demand for reward. It is caring as Jesus cared.

When we express such unencumbered compassion—no strings attached—needy people will be more prone to let us take them by the hand and help them. This applies to our helping the needy brother or sister sitting next to us in the pew. And it applies to our approach to the needy neighbor who has never met our Jesus.

True compassion is an expression of the life of our Lord Jesus Christ. It is always ready to give, and always willing to sacrifice. In an article entitled, "The Lavishness of Jesus," G. H. Morrison described this Christlike generosity:

> Love never asks how little can I do; . . . love always
> asks how much. Love does not merely go the measured
> mile; love travels to the uttermost. Love never haggles,
> never bargains, with "nicely calculated less or more."

Yes, compassion is generous, because it is the life of Jesus Christ flowing freely through us to others.

On Your Own

1. Carefully study the story of the good Samaritan, in Luke 10:30-37. Which person in the story best represents you? What do you see in the Samaritan's actions that you would like to emulate?

2. Is there someone who you know is in need but is difficult to show caring to, or perhaps is in a situation that has seemed too inconvenient for you to get involved in? Prayerfully decide what you could do to show love to that person. Do it!

4
The Badge of Discipleship

He drew a circle that shut me out—
heretic, rebel, a thing to flout.
But love and I had the wit to win—
we drew a circle that took him in.

I n his last tender moments with his followers before his arrest, Jesus shared some of the most significant teaching of the New Testament. He and the disciples had just celebrated the feast of the Passover together in an upper room in Jerusalem. They had also shared in the Lord's Supper, the bread and the fruit of the vine, which symbolized his suffering and death for us. Judas had left the little gathering to betray his Lord, and Jesus had turned his attention to the eleven who remained. What he shared with them, recorded in John 13:31–17:26, were to be guidelines for their lives and ministries in the years to come.

First among these significant teachings was a new impassioned appeal to love one another:

A new commandment I give to you, that you love one another, even as I have loved you, that you also love

one another. By this all men will know that you are my
disciples, if you have love for one another. (John 13:34-35)
The full significance of this command would challenge their
minds and grip their hearts after the resurrection. He had
been teaching them all along that love was the key. The great
lesson of love (Matthew 22:35-40) no doubt lingered in their
minds. Love for God had to come first, then love for their
neighbor would follow. However, here Jesus was calling for
love in the inner circle—among those who professed his name.

What he was saying to them was so important in our Savior's
mind that he called it a "new commandment." He was not just
offering them an option for one of the ways to make him
known. This commandment was in fact the key: Love is first.
Jesus made it very plain what kind of love he was talking
about: "even as I have loved you, that you also love one
another." This love is also a witness to the outsider. It clearly
identifies Christians with their Lord Jesus Christ. Francis
Schaeffer has commented on how significant this witness of
love is:

Love—and the unity it attests to—is the mark Christ
gave Christians to wear before the world. Only with
this mark may the world know that Christians are indeed
Christians and that Jesus was sent by the Father.[1]

¶ Jesus never wrote a book, yet the nature of his love was
indelibly impressed upon the minds of his followers. They
could never forget their three years experience with the Master.
He was the Model. His very life clearly defined love for them.
They had not only seen love embodied, but also experienced
it as they rubbed shoulders with the Savior. They observed
him as he moved with compassion among suffering people,
and they were personally blessed as they also were recipients
of his tender care.

What meaningful experiences must have flooded their minds

whenever they considered the command, "love one another, even as I have loved you." What glorious memories they had of his example of caring. And certainly every true believer should often recount such experiences of the Savior's love, especially in times of difficulty. How patient and caring he has been toward us, not only once, but again and again.

Peter, for example must have been deeply moved as he reflected upon the many times his Savior had given him special, loving consideration. He could never forget that his Master had taken time to visit his home in Capernaum, and how he and his family had been moved by the compassion Jesus had shown in healing his mother-in-law (Luke 4:38-39). Could Peter ever forget that the Savior really cared about his personal concerns, his family and his home? And then he would surely remember that the Master had promised to stand with him in his weakness on the spiritual battle line. The words were vividly impressed on his memory:

> Simon, Simon, behold, Satan has demanded permission to sift you like wheat; but I have prayed for you,
> that your faith may not fail; and you, when once you have turned again, strengthen your brothers. (Luke 22:31-32)

Every believer can be equally assured that the Savior stands with him lending his full, caring support by intercession when the spiritual battle is at its hottest (See Hebrews 7:25).

Then of course, Peter would always remember how he had failed his Lord. He had promised to be faithful to him to the end, even to die for him. But Peter discovered the emptiness of his own promises and the shame of his own failure when he denied his Master three times. Then, after just a knowing look from the Savior, Peter was so crushed with his failure that "he went out and wept bitterly" (Luke 22:62). If his story had ended there, Peter could never have been a victorious Christian, and he could never have preached the gospel. But he knew the forgiving love of his Savior. Peter would always cherish the first resurrection message the angel gave Mary Magdelene, and the other women, at the empty tomb: "But go, tell His disciples *and Peter* . . ." (Mark 16:7). Peter was forgiven, still numbered among chosen followers of the risen Savior. And we can identify with Peter. Each of us, in the honesty of our heart, can recall the guilt and the shame of utter failure. And, I hope, each of us can also testify to his compassionate forgiveness.

Perhaps most humbling of all Jesus' compassionate acts before Calvary was the foot-washing episode in the upper room, recorded in John 13:3-15. This event occurred just prior to the command to love one another. It is difficult for us to comprehend the Lord of Heaven taking on the role of a servant, but he did what was customary in Eastern homes for servants to do—wash the dusty feet of guests. One would assume that others of the group should have offered to perform this service. But Jesus' love was on display in this act of humility. John begins the chapter with the statement, "Jesus knowing that His hour had come that He should depart out of this world to the Father, having loved His own who were in the world, He loved them to the end" (verse 1). We could translate the last phrase, "He loved them to the uttermost." He gave himself completely to them. He could have demanded his rights and could have called on one of them to perform this humbling service, but he chose to serve them. And, remarkably, he chose to include Judas, who had already sold out to the devil (verse 2).

Again Peter especially could remember this experience. In his pride he almost missed the blessing: At first he would not allow Jesus to wash his feet. But Jesus patiently explained, and Peter submitted.

Peter and the others saw Jesus define love in unmistakable ways in his dealings with them. Let's summarize the important elements of this love:

- Jesus was concerned about their families, homes, and health.
- Jesus was willing to take time for people in need even though he was engaged in a busy ministry.
- Jesus provided faithful support in the spiritual battle by intercessory prayer.
- Jesus extended complete forgiveness, even when it seemed undeserved.
- Jesus humbly served his followers, exemplified in his washing their feet.
- Jesus ultimately gave himself in his death on Calvary's cross.

In all of these acts of compassion, Jesus modeled a practical brand of love. His was a love that ministered to his disciples' pressing needs. Calvary, of course, tied it all together: The cross dealt finally with their sins and opened the way for them to experience all the blessings of God. No example can ever measure up to the love of our Savior on the cross. But if the disciples were to "love one another, even as I have loved you," those experiences along the way would have to be etched in their minds as the examples to follow.

So it is with us. If we are to love our brothers and sisters as Jesus commanded, we must learn to express a practical love for the whole person. It must be the kind of love our Master has shown to us.

¶ If love is to be our badge of discipleship, how do we wear it? How do we display this important identification?

First we might ask, is it enough just to be nice to people? That is certainly a good start. Paul writes in Galatians 5:22 that love is a fruit of the spirit. And if we consider the fruit tree illustration suggested by this passage, we must acknowledge that fruit comes into view for all to see and appreciate. However, note that the fruit is on display whether those who observe it appreciate it or not; its genuineness lies in its constancy. Swiss leader Willard Becker has defined it for us: "False love is bound to its echo . . . [that is] bound to counter-love . . . [and] is dependent on moods and feelings. . . . Genuine love always has in it something of the nature of God's love. It is selfless and constant."[2]

The Christian is to love his brother whether or not his love is returned. He is, in fact, to be the first to initiate expressions of love, whether the climate seems favorable or not, rather than simply responding to others who love him. He loves because the love of Christ wells up in his heart, compelling him to express it. This is what it means to wear the badge of discipleship.

As a young man I discovered, quite by accident, how effective it could be to wear this badge of love. It was a wintry day in Detroit. I was trying to help a friend who had stalled his car in someone's driveway and was waiting for a tow truck. We kept trying to move the car but were making no progress. Meanwhile, the lady whose driveway was blocked by my friend's car angrily demanded that we move the car immediately or she would call the police. We tried to explain that we could do nothing until the tow truck arrived, but this did not satisfy her. She insisted that her husband was due home and that we must have the car moved before he arrived.

A few moments later the woman appeared again, this time with a shovel, and began to shovel her walk. Between strokes she would shout her displeasure at us, demanding again and again that we do the impossible—move the car. About this time I noticed that she wore only her house-dress, without a jacket, and was shivering in the cold. For some reason I felt compelled to help her. She refused, but I gently took the shovel and went to work, saying to her, "You'll catch cold without a jacket, and besides we have nothing to do but wait for the tow truck." At this the lady rather sheepishly slipped into the house, only to appear moments later with a more pleasant look on her face. She thanked me for shoveling her walk and then said, "You needn't worry about moving your car right away. My husband won't be home for at least two hours." The badge of love had done its work!

¶ Those who followed the Master not only practiced this caring love but also urged others to do the same. Peter, for example, indicated that he had learned the lesson well. Thus he wrote, "Above all, keep fervent in your love for one another, because love covers a multitude of sins" (1 Peter 4:8). Our love for each other must be fervent and intense. Peter knew exactly what this meant. Jesus had demonstrated this kind of love to him. William Barclay says that Peter's term, "fervent," has two meanings: 1) outstretching in the sense of consistency; our love must be the kind that never fails, and 2) stretching out as a runner stretches out; our love must be energetic. Barclay comments further, "It means loving the unlovely and the unlovable; it means loving in spite of insult and injury, it means loving when love is not returned."[3] Peter says this kind of love "covers a multitude of sins." Our love can overlook the sins of our brother. The writer of Proverbs says, "Love covers all transgressions" (10:12). Thus the Christian is enabled by the love of God to overlook another person's faults, and even to bear with his foolishness and endure his unkindness.

John also caught the vision and passed on the command in his love chapter: "Beloved, if God so loved us, we also ought to love one another" (1 John 4:11). Then Paul, who joined the apostolic ranks later, beautifully defined the practice of love in the supreme chapter on the subject, 1 Corinthians 13. To Paul, the badge we wear is just a tin badge if it is not the obvious control of divine *(agape)* love in our lives. This kind of love never fails, and is the greatest of all virtues.

New Testament caring is not easy. It demands that we give ourselves wholly to God, then to our brothers and sisters. John Powell calls for this kind of dedication when he discusses "the meaning of love":

> Whatever else can and should be said of love, it is quite evident that true love demands self-forgetfulness. . . . this is the test: Can we really forget ourselves?[4]

Powell goes on to state that there are many counterfeit products on the market. We can even deceive ourselves into thinking we are showing love when we are actually meeting our own needs; that is, we are receiving some personal gratification by expressing love (as we might say) to another. But "the acid test," Powell says, "is always the probing question of self-forgetfulness."[5]

The apostle John reveals the answer to this difficult qualification when he quotes the Savior as saying, "Truly, truly, I say to you, unless a grain of wheat falls into the earth and dies, it remains by itself alone; but if it dies, it bears much fruit" (John 12:24). In this passage, Jesus states the requirements for discipleship. He is saying that we must deal with all of the ugly, self-centered characteristics of our lives by putting them to death. The self-life, or the "flesh," cannot in any sense be a vehicle to express the love of Christ. We must give God the freedom to deal with this sin nature of ours so that the love of Jesus Christ may be expressed through us.

Self-forgetfulness becomes a reality when our lives are totally under the Savior's control. He can then love others through us, so what is impossible in human strength becomes possible by the power of his life in us. This is the only way we as weak human beings can love our brothers—the only way we can love the one who is difficult, or the one we are not naturally drawn to. It is not our love being expressed to others, but, as Christ's agents, it is his love in and through us. Only in this way can we love others as he loved us.

On Your Own

1. What characteristics of humble caring or servanthood did Jesus display in John 13:1-15?

2. Pray over this example and decide how you could show this same caring to someone you know to be in need. Do it!

PART TWO
Transforming the Local Body

5
Finding and Healing Hurts

How much unnoticed suffering goes on in our churches? How many are crying out for help without being heard? How loudly does one have to cry? A cartoon from the "Winnie the Pooh" comic strip perhaps reveals how insensitive we often are. Pooh Bear is walking along a river bank while Eeyore (the stuffed donkey) is floating downstream on his back:

Pooh—"Did you fall into the river, Eeyore?"

Eeyore—"Silly of me, wasn't it?"

Pooh—"Is the river uncomfortable this morning?"

Eeyore—"Well yes, the dampness you know."

Pooh—"You really ought to be more careful!"

Eeyore—"Thanks for the advice."

Pooh—"I think you're sinking."

Eeyore—"Pooh, if it's not too much trouble, would you mind rescuing me?"

Eeyore (as he is being pulled out)—"I'm sorry to be such a bother."

Pooh—"Don't be silly, Eeyore. You should have said something sooner."

Could this scene describe some of our churches? Do we find ourselves seeing our fellow believers in need but doing nothing about it? If my church is anywhere near average, it appears that this is a common problem.

How often we engage in conversation about—or with—a suffering person, but somehow manage not to get involved. We may even ask them how they are doing and verbally express our concern. Perhaps we even go to the extreme of offering to help. "Just give me a call," we may say. We know of course that such a call will never come, even though we meant it sincerely. People are reluctant to ask for help—even suffering people. Yet they send out signals that indicate they are in need. Surprisingly, as with Pooh, we don't seem to heed their signals until they get desperate. Then we might say, "Why didn't you say something sooner?"

Can you imagine, for example, a housewife appearing in church on Sunday morning with her right arm in a cast? Several people stop her and ask, "Did you break your arm?" She says yes. Some pursue it further, perhaps commenting, "It must be difficult doing your housework with that cast on your arm." Again she nods agreement. But let's suppose that she is a woman of courage, and that she asks one of her would-be sympathizers, "Would you mind coming over on Monday morning to help me with the washing and ironing?" We know, of course, that she is not likely to make such a bold request. In fact, most people are reluctant even to mention their needs, let alone ask for help. But if this woman were to ask, would she receive the help she needs?

Strangely, in what is supposed to be a loving, caring fellowship, there are few who seem able to mention (even for prayer) that they are suffering. Writer Orien Johnson, puzzled by this, asked why people don't open up in our churches. He has suggested five reasons for why people tend to keep their problems to themselves:

1. The usual church services are not designed for this.
2. We feel it is a sign of weakness to admit we have problems.
3. We feel also that it is a reflection on our faith to have problems.
4. Our relationships in the church are not deep enough.
5. Finally, we feel that it just wouldn't do any good to tell anyone about our problems.[1]

What conclusions can we draw from such observations? First, we must admit they are true. Johnson's reasons are valid for many of our churches. Second, most churches are not the healing communities they ought to be.

Sometimes the signals people give, though not verbal, are as obvious as the cast on a broken arm. Other times, however, they are very subtle. In either case the person may be trying to say, "I hurt, won't anybody help?" He may withdraw and become unusually quiet, or he may become very talkative and almost hyperactive. One may become very passive, another argumentative and angry. Whatever the signals, a loving fellowship ought to be the place in which they will be recognized and responded to. In fact, there ought to be freedom to give open, verbal expression to our hurts to at least one other person in the fellowship of believers.

¶ The local church is the body of Christ in a given community. The characteristics of that body should be visible there.

Ray Stedman, pastor of the Peninsula Bible Church of Palo Alto, California, is known for his pioneering in the body life concept in the local church. He aptly describes the wonder of a living body:

A body is formed by the extension of one original cell which grows until it becomes a mature body in which every cell shares the original life. That is the secret of a body—all parts of it share life together.[2]

Stedman comments further that "it is the sharing of life that makes a body different from an organization."[3] We know from the New Testament that the church is not merely an organization, it is a body! And since it is a body, all members share mutually in its life. As Stedman states so well,

The church is primarily and fundamentally a body designed to express through each individual member the life of an indwelling Lord and is equipped by the Holy Spirit with gifts designed to express that life.[4]

This picture is clearly portrayed for us in 1 Corinthians 12. Here we are taught that a prominent feature of such a living organism is its unity. Though there are many members, they function in harmony, for they are actually one. Jesus Christ himself is the Head (see Colossians 1:18). The members of the body, therefore, are to respond quickly and willingly to his every command. If each member were to do his own thing the body would be spastic. Every movement would require great effort but would result only in misspent energy and failure. The members of the body would then be reluctant to minister to one another. If our Savior is indeed in charge, however, there will be a sharing of suffering, sharing of honor, and a sharing of joy.

A local church experiencing such body life is a beautiful sight. In fact, where even a few members begin to understand such mutual caring, it has a marked effect upon the entire assembly of believers.

¶ True Christian fellowship is more than a gathering around coffee and donuts. The New Testament word for it is *koinonia;* it means to share something in common with others. This common bond and focal point that draws us together is our Lord Jesus Christ himself. When we have become sharers in his love we are drawn to others who are objects of that same love. This happens because the Holy Spirit is loving through us. As human beings we are made to respond to love; when we are born of the Spirit, this sharing becomes a possibility.

This is the answer to life's needs which the world is looking for. The church *does* have the answer. Simply declaring it is useless, however; we must *demonstrate* it within our own ranks. As Francis Schaeffer has said,

There is no use saying you have community or love for each other if it does not get down into the tough stuff of life. It must, or we are producing ugliness in the name of truth. I am convinced that in the 20th century people all over the world will not listen if we have the right doctrine, the right polity, but are not exhibiting community.[5]

We as Christians have a meaningful, life-changing relationship with a caring God. But we must let God have freedom in our fellowships to teach us how to have meaningful relationships with one another. This is the community Schaeffer calls for—a practical relationship of love. The fellowship is expressed not only in talking to one another, but also in actually helping one another. When this happens in a local assembly, the church grows. It is healthy. Elton Trueblood declares that such fellowship will stimulate Christian service:

The renewal of the church will be in progress when it is seen as a fellowship of consciously inadequate persons who gather because they are weak, and scatter to serve because their unity with one another and with Christ has made them bold.[6]

The difference Christ makes must begin to show within the ranks of believers. Then it cannot help but spill over into the outside world.

¶ How often have we sat in our pew on Sunday morning doing our best to concentrate on worshiping the Lord but remaining totally unaware of the needs all around us?

Joyce Landorf tells of having this kind of experience one Sunday morning as she sat in the choir loft. A note was passed to her that read, "See the couple in the fifth row of the west auditorium, aisle seats? He has on a navy blue suit and she is dressed in lavender. Their marriage is over. Pray for them; they need a miracle!" Joyce noted that the couple were listening attentively to the sermon, but without any expression—not even a nod or smile. How long had they been suffering in deep need and hurt? Mrs. Landorf prayed for them, and then wondered about the people seated behind and to the left of them. "Do they need a miracle too?" she pondered. Then she began to ask for whatever miracle this one or that one needed.[7] This is a good starting place for expressing caring—prayer.

Somehow the body of believers must get involved in each other's lives! We can start with the average Christian in the pew—we must help him become a caring person. He must become aware of the needs, be alert to the signals people give, and learn some skills in offering a helping hand. This can be done at the friendship level. Paul Welter, a professor of counseling at Kearney State College in Nebraska, underlines the need for a friend helping a friend:

> There is a need today to prepare more people so they can help their friends. We need to have competent persons "at the scene of the accident." To carry the medical analogy further, helpers can give psychological first aid, but they can do far more than this—they can make long-term positive differences in the lives of the persons they help. A person who reaches out to help someone who is . . . close already has met the first prerequisite of successful caring—a friendly relationship.[8]

¶ It is this friendly relationship, which already existed to a degree, that we wanted to capitalize on within our church family. The door was already open, at least a crack, to enter the life of a brother or sister and say, "I care." With this in mind, we began to train people to care for their peers. Our people entered these training classes with great anticipation, and as they learned and began to practice what they learned, their enthusiasm grew. The people in this group said they volunteered because they wanted to learn to help people who were hurting but felt inadequate to do so. One church leader commented, "I need to learn how to get out of myself and get genuinely involved and interested in others." A young wife remarked, "I especially hope to improve my skill in counseling and talking with wives of alcoholics. Also, I feel the class would help me deal with our foster child in a more effective way." Said still another, a businessman, "It is easy for me to care for others. The Lord has dealt with me in this area but I still have a long way to go."

We knew that in order to reach such goals as these, this group could not be a typical Sunday school class—it had to be an on-the-job training unit. We kept the group small at first; later training classes were slightly larger. The curriculum included a careful study of the New Testament principles of caring. Each member of the group selected a needy person in the church to care for during the thirteen-week training period.

It was exciting to see the results God gave us in this first meager attempt to grow as a caring church. Each member of the class testified to having grown in his grasp of both the concept and the skills of caring for those in need, and all but one said they wanted to continue the ministry they had begun.

It was equally gratifying to see results in the lives of those who were on the receiving end. One class member chose to care for an elderly woman whose husband was an alcoholic. This man professed to be a Christian but had been very abusive toward his wife. The woman trainee had come from a similar set of circumstances but had experienced a greater degree of victory. She spent a great deal of time encouraging the older woman, both on the telephone and by her visits in the home. The older woman had become very bitter toward her husband but was reaching out for love and reassurance. The trainee also helped by providing transportation to the doctor's office, a round trip of about fifty miles. When the alcoholic husband was hospitalized to overcome his habit, his wife at first said she would not take him back home again. As a result of the encouragement she was receiving, however, she relented. She received him with kindness and offered to work with him in an attempt to save their marriage.

As these on-the-job caring classes have been repeated over the past few years, many people have observed that our church is growing as a caring, healing fellowship. We have been realizing our goals. We've taken this as a signal not to quit, however, but as an encouragement to press on with what we are doing.

On Your Own

1. Read carefully 1 Corinthians 12 and Colossians 1:18. If the church is a body with Christ as the Head, what should characterize the body life or fellowship of the church?

2. As you sit in church next Sunday waiting fo the service to begin, try praying for people around you who seem lonely or burdened. Then make it a point to talk to at least one of those people after the service. Listen to him or her with interest, and, if you feel free to do so, offer some word of encouragement.

6
Becoming a Family

M ost of us like the idea of being cared for. We want others to show interest in us. But how many of us spontaneously go out of our way to care for others? Here is where many of our churches are noticeably weak. We've all heard or made comments about unfriendly churches. But it isn't churches that are friendly or unfriendly, it's individuals. For this reason many churches have official greeters who welcome people as they walk through the church doors each Sunday. This is a good beginning; people do respond to a friendly face, a warm handshake, or a kind word. They want to know that someone is glad to see them.

But official greeters are only a beginning, because what people really want is genuine friendship and acceptance. It is possible to greet someone at the front door but never let him in—to our church, our home, our life. A brief greeting takes just moments; letting someone in means getting involved. This is where many of us draw the line. They will not sacrifice the time—for it does take time to be truly friendly. They will not put forth the effort—and it does take effort to listen and share. They will not take the risk—and there is risk in exposing oneself to the intimacy of continuing friendship.

A young single who had recently joined our church told us that from his first encounter he had been impressed with the friendliness of our people. In his testimony he recalled how he'd been a part of the drug culture but recently opened his heart to the Lord. He moved to our community to begin a new job in the engineering field. Though he was successful professionally, he was very lonely and hungry for a church where he could be fed spiritually and find encouraging Christian fellowship. From the first Sunday he was invited into the homes of our people. He also found there were others who had come to Christ out of a similar background, and so he had an immediate affinity with people who understood his needs. He got involved in a Bible study and found a prayer partner. Just after that he ran into some problems on the job, and he was deeply troubled by pressure from his boss. He immediately found, however, that he had a support team of men who shared his burden and backed him in prayer. Three or four weeks later he was able to report how God had dealt with the problem. He was rejoicing in the victory, and he said that this was one of the most significant experiences he'd had as a Christian. It is this kind of friendship that makes a church a caring fellowship.

¶ The local community of believers should be characterized by a family spirit—a bond of love that can be understood only by those who experience it. A middle-aged man who came to Christ during his wife's serious illness found himself surrounded by this spirit. His wife's beautiful testimony had been the key factor in his conversion; it was perhaps incidental that a pastor happened to be present in the hospital room when he yielded his life to the Lord just before his wife was wheeled off to heart surgery. During the months of her recovery he was overwhelmed by the church family's loving concern. Visitors brought food, cleaned their house, and stopped by just to encourage them. When his wife suddenly died of a massive heart attack, he again experienced a warm, generous response from God's people. At a family pot-luck dinner following the memorial service, he commented to the pastor on the large gathering that day and the closeness of his family ties. Then he added, "The church is like this, only more so. It's just like a big family."

One of the characteristics of family life that so attracted this man was the loving care Christians displayed for one another. The apostle Paul (as well as other New Testament writers) frequently makes this point by using the expression, "one another." He uses this phrase several times in Romans 12-15. It speaks of the special relationship and closeness God had in mind for believers in the local body, or fellowship of believers. It is not like a club membership; neither is it like a casual social gathering. Rather, there is a special bond of love that surpasses all other human relationships (apart from marriage) for its closeness. For example, Paul tells the believers at Rome that we are "members one of another" (12:5). He uses an analogy to the human body to illustrate the nature and function of the church. Though we are individuals, each with different gifts, we share in the life of the body—the local church. This "one another" principle (as some have called it) says that we belong to each other. We cannot function adequately or grow to maturity unless we are wholeheartedly committed to a fellowship of believers and actively sharing our lives with them (see Ephesians 4:15-16).

A second way in which Paul uses this "one another" principle in Romans is by commanding to "be devoted to one another in brotherly love" (12:10). Since we are a part of God's family, the warmth and mutual concern of healthy family life should be a part of church life.

Paul uses this principle a third time when he asks us to "give preference to one another in honor" (Romans 12:10). This selflessness is also part of healthy family life. Paul expands on this idea in his letter to the Philippians: "Do nothing from selfish or empty conceit, but with humility of mind let each of you regard one another as more important than himself; do not merely look out for your own personal interests, but also for the interests of others" (2:3-4). Striving for position or the praise of men is acting selfishly. Seeking the advancement and happiness of others is exhibiting the love of Christ.

The fourth "one another" in this section of Romans tells us that "we are to be of the same mind with one another" (15:5), referring to the unity that results from a clear understanding of the body principle. And fifth, Paul says we are to "accept one another" (15:7). This is the first step in caring in the local church. Those who begin to attend our fellowships want to be accepted unconditionally. Too often, many of our churches have accepted new people only if they measured up to an arbitrary set of standards: dress, hair, and lifestyle had to coincide with a legalistic profile. But the Scriptures say, "accept the one who is weak in faith, but not for the purpose of passing judgment on his opinions" (Romans 14:1). This is not countenancing sin; it is simply a matter of receiving and loving those for whom Christ died.

Paul also tells us in Romans that we are to "admonish one another" (15:14). This is a difficult requirement. The Greek term "admonish" used here means to speak a word of encouragement to help correct another Christian, without provoking or embittering him. Paul used the same term when he spoke of his relationship to the Ephesian church: "remembering that night and day for a period of three years I did not cease to admonish each one with tears " (Acts 20:31). Admonition is a form of spiritual counseling, requiring godly love from those who are giving it as well as from those who are receiving it. When the "one another" relationship has grown to this point, love has become the rule. The church has truly become a caring family.

I learned the importance of this principle from two laymen in my first church. We were involved in a building program at the time, and work had reached a stage in which weariness and frayed tempers had begun to show. These two men had roughed in some plumbing, but then the plans changed and they had to do part of the job over. The reworking created tensions, and the men began to attack each other with verbal barrages. They ended up dropping their tools and storming off to their homes.

As a young, idealistic pastor, I was unsure of what I should do. After prayer, however, I realized I had to admonish each man in love. Both of them were to teach Sunday school the next day, but I knew that neither was prepared to be used of God after their argument. So, with fear and trembling, I called first one and then the other, giving each the same message. After telling them I had heard the whole argument, I asked, "Don't you think you owe your brother an apology? Do you think you can possibly be effective with your class tomorrow in this frame of mind?"

Each man responded beautifully, showing his maturity in Christ. They both shared with me the next day about how one had gone to the other's home, and how they had patched things up with proper apologies, forgiveness, and prayer.

The kind of church people are attracted to is a "one another" fellowship: where, in the discipline of love, each cares for the other and is open enough to admonish and be admonished—a church in which people share their lives.

¶ Dr. Gary Collins describes the remarkable phenomenon of the body of believers as a healing community.[1] He points out that psychologists have discovered the effectiveness of group helping, which they call "milieu therapy." In this kind of therapy, a group lives, works, and plays together, and everyone has some responsibility. The group is characterized by open communication, and an atmosphere of "openness, honesty, warmth, acceptance, and inter-personal caring."

Collins points out that God provided just such a healing community long ago—the local church. As individuals help individuals, they collectively have the dynamic impact of a vital, caring group. Our churches can and should be groups such as this. Obviously, the pastor alone cannot accomplish it. True, he must lead the way and be a model of such caring, personally as well as in his pulpit ministry, as he skillfully applies biblical truth as a healing balm to the hurts of his people. But it takes the whole congregation working together to produce a healing fellowship.

We must find a way in our churches for everyone to get involved. The average Christian must be convinced that though the pastor provides the primary leadership, every member of the church can be a part of the ministry of caring. David Dunston, an expert in lay ministries, has commented, "There is a need to convince working class Christians that they are trusted and respected. People who have grown used to the idea that they are the ones to be led, rather than the leaders, need to be convinced of their value."[2]

The layman has a distinct advantage in person-to-person ministries such as evangelism, discipling, and caring, because he has contacts the pastor may never reach. Every faithful Christian, for example, has a circle of friends he can share with and encourage. Collins calls such encouragers "peer helpers." He insists, wisely, that they can accomplish what trained professionals may not be able to do:

In contrast to professionals the peer helper (a) is closer to the helpee, knows him as a friend, and is thus better able to understand his problem and pick up non-verbal clues or to demonstrate a sincere empathy; (b) is more often available and is thus able to provide help consistently and whenever it is especially needed; (c) often knows about the helpee's family, work situation, life-style, beliefs, or neighborhood and can therefore take a more active part in guiding decisions or helping the helpee to change his life situation; (d) is able to communicate in language . . . which the helpee can easily understand; and (e) is more down to earth, relaxed, open, informal, and inclined to introduce a tension-relieving humor.[3]

We saw the potential that every Christian has for a ministry to his or her peers develop in the caring ministry in our church. Each person in our training classes selected at least one person to care for, most often someone with whom they could easily communicate and for whom they felt God had given them a burden.

This "peer helper" concept was beautifully illustrated by a young wife who chose to encourage a young woman new in the church. The new woman's husband was an alcoholic, and her family was experiencing the stresses common to this kind of problem. It seemed evident that the Lord had chosen the encourager, because our worker had also experienced the stresses and heartache of a disrupted home—her mother was in the advanced stages of alcoholism. She understood the problem and the helpless feeling of watching a loved one destroy her life while refusing to admit she had a problem. Our caring worker was able to be a positive influence in the life of the new member, and they spent a great deal of time sharing and praying, on the telephone as well as face to face. And so one new, suffering member was stabilized by a peer helper who understood and cared. This new member is now an effective worker in our Sunday school. Her husband's problem is not yet solved, but she is learning to be strong in the Lord in spite of it.

On Your Own

1. Read carefully John 12:23-26 and Philippians 2:3-4. What is involved in submitting yourself to others? Try to answer in terms of attitudes, actions, and commitment.

2. Based upon Romans 12:9-16 and Galatians 6:1-2, how did Paul instruct Christians to care for one another?

3. As you review the verses above, does anything stand out to you as a need in your life which you would like to work on so that God can use you in the life of another person? If so, write it down so you won't forget about it. This week, make it a point to pray over this need, asking God for the sanctifying work of the Holy Spirit in this area of your life.

7
Learning How to Care

T oday while my back was turned, somebody reassuredly grasped my arm unexpectedly. It was you. It was the extra something I needed. Thanks a lot."[1]

A Midwestern pastor received this note of thanks from a recently widowed woman in his congregation. A small display of thoughtfulness and concern had meant a great deal to her at a time of need. The same pastor later commented, "There's so little time anymore to touch anybody. There are so few moments to hug and to hold on. There are only a few unsteady seconds for stopping to look anyone straight in the eye."[2] It's too bad the church didn't come up with the line, "Reach out and touch someone," before Ma Bell did. This ought to be one of our key slogans.

Touching may not be the total answer, but it can be very significant in expressing our care for others. Pastor Leslie

B. Flynn comments on the need for this, pointing out that the early church's custom was to greet one another with a "holy kiss" (for example, see Romans 16:16). Flynn reminds us that the need for touch begins in infancy:

> Psychological tests reveal that infants who are not touched lovingly suffer emotional deprivation as adults. A baby should be kissed, hugged, held and touched every day.

Flynn goes on to comment that we need this kind of attention throughout life:

> But the basic need to be touched and comforted continues through life. One counselor advises holding your child on your lap if you're watching TV unless he's bigger than you are, ruffling your son's hair or patting his arm as you pass by, or giving him a kiss goodnight. Perhaps the entire family needs to be more physically affectionate. Older folks need to be touched also, as well as the ill. Experiments show that people in deep comas often show improved heart rates when their hands are held by doctors or nurses.[3]

We too often miss the mark in showing genuine concern to others. At times we may be too casual, too flippant, or just plain cold and distant. Christians must learn to communicate with each other in ways that express the love of Christ. Such expressions, however, should be natural and meaningful, not forced. Touch may come more easily for some than for others. In prayer we should ask, "How can I best express encouragement and reassurance without being misunderstood?" The answer the Lord gives will probably differ with each individual.

There are certain cautions we should heed in this area. First, our motives must be right. Our aim must clearly be to honor the Lord and to be a vehicle through which he can express his love. If you sense an ulterior motive in your desire to be expressive, the wisest course is not to do it! Second, treat touch between the sexes with discretion. If there are any sexual overtones, it is best to stay away from the situation. We need to remember at all times that our goal in expressing care to others is to convey an unmistakable message of Christian love.

¶ Whether or not we are able to sincerely show Christian love by touch, we need to find ways to have closer relationships to our brothers and sisters in Christ. Thomas Dubay insists that real caring cannot take place until we've gotten close enough to see and understand the other person's needs: "To care is to jump into the other's skin. It is to become the other in mind and heart, to live the other's interests. To care is to become one's brother, one's sister."[4]

Caring for our brothers and sisters does not mean we are any better than they are. We can easily identify with their needs for comfort and help because we've been there too. Evangelism has been defined as "one beggar telling another beggar where to find bread." Caring is one sufferer telling another sufferer where to find comfort.

The apostle Paul seems to be speaking about becoming God's instrument of help in 2 Corinthians 1:3-7. He uses the term "comfort" ten times in this short passage. The Greek root in this word is the same one used in names for Jesus Christ and the Holy Spirit (for example, see John 14:16-18, 14:26, and 16:7). The Holy Spirit is our "Comforter" or "Helper," one who comes alongside to help another, consoling or comforting him. Unless we deliberately get close enough to make a real offer of help, with concern and compassion, we are just mouthing words. Hurting people are quick to sense when our hearts are not in it.

This passage in 2 Corinthians 1 provides another essential clue to becoming an instrument of God's help. Paul describes a comfort that originates with God himself. Please note that *God* is finally and essentially the Comforter. He is "the Father of mercies and God of all comfort" (verse 3). Paul notes that God "comforts us in all our affliction" (verse 4). As Paul indicates in this passage, however, God's purpose in comforting us, or coming alongside to help us, is not an end in itself. He intends that we pass it on. Whatever God gives us is not only for our benefit, but also to prepare us to share with others: It is his purpose that we become comforters and encouragers. This is clear especially in verse 4, where we're told that he "comforts us in all our affliction—*so that we may be able to comfort those who are in any affliction with the comfort with which we ourselves are comforted by God.*"

It seems that the qualification to be an encourager of others is to have personally experienced God's comfort and encouragement. Many in the world offer care at the human level only—philanthropic organizations, for example. The Christian, however, has a great deal more to offer. But in order to be effective, he must be living in close fellowship with God. He must know by experience that God meets his most pressing needs: then he will be compelled to share what God has given him. Here is where spiritual experience translates into practical reality. And as we share in a practical way with others, our own appreciation of God's blessings will be more vivid than ever.

¶ Robert Schuller, widely known in Christian circles as a pastor and television preacher, writes of the successful caring groups his church has developed. The congregation is divided into geographic zones, with eight families in each group. Each member reports weekly to his or her group leader. Schuller says they first learn to practice love on each other by following seven principles:

1. Learn to lose ourselves in others.
2. Learn to listen deeply.
3. Learn to love the unlovely.

4. Learn to leave our mistakes at the foot of the cross.
5. Learn how to discover God's plan for our lives.
6. Learn to lean on the power of the Holy Spirit.
7. Learn to lead others to Christ.[5]

This is good, practical advice for getting close to and caring for people. We have used some of these same principles in our own caring program, and the results have been changed lives—among our workers as well as those being helped. This principle of reciprocal blessing is always at work when we give ourselves in ministry to others. One person who was helping an elderly woman said, "I have received so much more than I have given. She has been such a blessing to me!" The joy we receive in giving ourselves to others can far outweigh sacrifices we may have to make.

We have found five principles to be of critical significance in our church caring program. Each is an important step in drawing close to another person and having an effective ministry.

The first important principle is *prayer.* All effective ministry begins with prayer, involving at least three aspects: the *prayer of preparation;* second, the *prayer for direction;* and third, the *prayer of intercession.* Each is critically important. We need to begin with a prayer of preparation because our human hearts do not naturally reach out to others. Because of our tendency to be concerned only with ourselves, we must draw near to God and learn of love from him. It helps to review how much he loves us by praying over verses such as John 3:16 and 15:13, Romans 5:8, and 1 John 4:10-11. As we thank God for his love for us, we can begin to pray for a love for others.

After preparing our hearts, we can follow up with a prayer for direction. A look around our church fellowship (we asked our people to begin their ministry of caring in the local church) can quickly reveal those in need. We then need to ask God to show us the one to whom we should minister.

Once we receive direction, we move on to the most important aspect of prayer in ministry: intercession. This was one of Hudson Taylor's secrets of success in his ministry in China. "It is possible to move men, through God," Taylor said, "by prayer alone." The apostle Paul recognized a man named Epaphras for such intercessory prayer for the Christians at Colossae:

> Epaphras, who is one of your number, a bondslave of Jesus Christ, sends you his greetings, always laboring earnestly for you in his prayers, that you may stand perfect and fully assured in all the will of God.
> (Colossians 4:12)

A caring ministry begins in prayer, is sustained by prayer, and succeeds by prayer. Ministry attempted by any other approach quickly becomes an activity of the flesh and is doomed to failure.

The second principle we have found necessary for a direct caring ministry is contact. This is one reason God left us in the world after we were saved. In his high-priestly prayer in John 17, Jesus asked on behalf of his followers, "I do not ask Thee to take them out of the world, but to keep them from the evil one" (verse 15). As our Savior's representatives, we are to be God's instruments of blessing—his hands, his feet, his voice. Most believers have plenty of contact with people, but it is often virtually meaningless in expanding the Kingdom of God. We are in the world to have purposeful contact with needy people, so that God can use us as his ministers of mercy.

We need to be careful, however, not to approach the person we have prayed for too aggressively. Our aim should be to build a bridge of friendship, with caution and gentleness, which we can cross over to minister to his needs. This may take time: some people will not open up until we have earned their trust with our friendship.

Casual conversations, perhaps before or after a church

service, provide ideal first contacts. Be prepared for the relationship to develop slowly. An invitation to your home or to go out for coffee after the Sunday evening service will often open the door. Occasional, short phone conversations are also a good means of showing interest. One elderly lady in our fellowship puts many of us to shame in these avenues to caring. Although she is seldom able to attend church services because of illness, she prays for many in the congregation, including children, and each one by name. Since she has a special concern for those her own age, she often calls them to offer encouragement, telling of God's faithfulness to her or sharing a verse that is a current blessing. Sometimes this lady will share some of her own poetry, always the product of some recent experience of God's provision and blessing. In response, her elderly friends will call her when they are discouraged. They find that it is uplifting just to talk to her on the phone.

A third key principle in caring is *listening.* We warn our people not to be self-styled counselors, and to be slow to give advice. Many times just being there is sufficient. Sometimes the needy person may not even want to talk, but when he does it is very important to listen with interest, giving our undivided attention as he unburdens his heart. We'll be discussing this important skill in more detail in the next chapter.

The fourth principle we use in our church caring program is *helping*—the voluntary giving of ourselves. Help is costly. It can involve, for example, giving time—and this can be the most costly gift of all. Many times we'd much rather speak a word of greeting, send a card, or give some money. But time is a precious commodity in our busy culture, and we are often reluctant to give it up—even though it is often the very gift that best says, "I care."

Along with time are the companion gifts of energy, and performing a task that lifts the load for a needy person. The significance here often lies not just in the gift itself, but also in the message it conveys. The following story has been told of an encounter that makes just this point:

> Sleet was falling and it was slushy under foot. People hurried homeward with their coat collars up, hardly glancing at others who passed by. A young black man, carrying a heavy valise in one hand, a huge suitcase in the other, was slipping and sliding as he rushed toward Grand Central Station. Suddenly a hand reached out and took one of his bags, and a pleasant voice said, "Let me have that, Brother. In this bad weather it's hard to carry so much!" At first the man was reluctant, but the smile of his would-be friend put him at ease. Soon they were walking together, chatting like two old buddies. Years later Booker T. Washington said, "That kindly deed was my introduction to Theodore Roosevelt."

To the person on the receiving end, a caring deed is the mark of greatness. Christians above all should be known for such acts of kindness. As our caring ministry grew, we were greatly encouraged to see this kind of helping take place with increasing frequency. One lady began to call on an elderly Christian woman with a heart ailment. When she discovered the suffering woman's physical limitations, she began to telephone regularly to say, "I'd like to come over tomorrow to do your housework for you." Needless to say, the older woman gladly accepted this practical help. Not only did it lift her load, but it gave her a new joy and assurance that someone cared.

The fifth principle we have found to be essential to a caring ministry is *encouragement*. Although it is inherent in the other four principles, it is necessary for the caring person to be thinking specifically along these lines. The result will be deliberate, thoughtful expressions intended to uplift the other person—whether face to face, by telephone, a written note, or even in a carefully selected greeting card. The encouragement may take the form of a compliment, a thank-you for a task well done, or just a spontaneous "thinking of you."

I was reminded of how important this kind of encouragement can be when I heard of a woman who, while sorting through her deceased mother's possessions, came across a card she'd sent her mother years ago. The card read, "This morning when I wakened and saw the sun above, I softly said, 'Good morning, Lord, bless everyone I love!' Right away I thought of you. . . ." The woman was surprised to find that her mother had been keeping the card in her Bible all those years, treasuring her daughter's gesture of loving concern.

Encouragement does not preach or push. It is often a spontaneous word from the overflow of a loving heart, springing up naturally as we share our lives with others.

¶ When visiting a man with terminal cancer I commented upon leaving, "We really care about you." He immediately responded, "The people at the church are so loving and kind," and his wife quickly echoed him. This kind of response to our church fellowship seems to be expressed more and more often, and this has been a great encouragement and also a stimulus to keep on caring. We cannot be sure that any particular facet of our caring ministry is going to be a model for other churches, but we have found the following approaches to be helpful in our congregation.

1. *Greeting and fellowship.* Even though they've been through our training class, some people do not feel they can have a regular ministry of caring. However, they have been willing to function as greeters, who welcome those attending our services. Others seem to find it easier to converse with people informally in the sanctuary following the regular services. Consequently, the church empties more slowly now—which is an indicator of good health.

2. *One-on-one.* Personal caring is, of course, ideal. Some people do this spontaneously, while others ask to be assigned to help another person. This approach has developed considerably in our church under the leadership of a woman with training in home nursing care, who has developed a three-phase program: 1) Personal care, 2) Homemaking care, and 3) Supportive care. The first phase requires nurse's aid training and includes functions an aide would perform in a hospital. The second involves household chores and handyman repairs. The third phase includes occasional visits, sending greeting cards, and so forth. All of these workers are concerned with the whole person and are available to pray with or read the Scriptures to him. A chairperson coordinates all one-on-one caring ministries.

3. *Care and share.* A group of workers meets weekly to share with and encourage each other and to continue to sharpen their caring skills. They keep up with caring needs in the church and pray regularly about them. They also volunteer to do one-on-one caring.

4. *Deacons' shepherding.* Our emphasis on caring has caused our Deacons to reconsider their shepherding responsibilities. Each Deacon is asked to take the Caring Training Class, and then to shepherd his segment of the congregation with this teaching to guide him. He is given three to four assistants to work with him in his duties as a shepherd.

Whatever the approach, it is clear that the local church ought to be a caring fellowship. Body life, as Paul describes it, requires "that the members should have the same care for one another" (1 Corinthians 12:25).

On Your Own

1. Write down the instructions that Paul gives on comfort, or encouragement, in 2 Corinthians 1:3-7. Try to

find the source, the purpose, and the example of comfort in this passage.

2. Review the five key principles for caring for others that are listed in this chapter. Select one of these principles that you would like to develop in your life. Feel free to start off with an area that is personally appealing to you.

8
Adopting a Spirit of Gentleness

P eople are a lot like eggs," it's been said. "We may look tough on the outside, but we're pretty easily cracked."[1] We recognize this fragile condition in ourselves and long to be treated with tenderness, but we do not often remember that others have the same need. Sometimes it seems that we treat others the way a postal clerk would who was processing a package that read, "Contents uncertain: Handle with nonchalance"! We are often so preoccupied with our concerns that we are too busy—or too careless—to notice the needs of those who cross our path.

We need to learn how to adopt a spirit of gentle concern for others. Paul Welter appropriately asks, "Are helpers only to be soft? Are there two kinds of persons, the tender helper type, and the hard leader type?" The answer is no: even the tough leader must be tender in his dealings with people. That is the way God treats us. Recall, for example, his great tenderness and sensitivity to our needs, expressed in Psalm 103:13-14: "Just as a father has compassion on his children, So the Lord has compassion on those who fear Him. For He Himself knows our frame; He is mindful that we are but dust."

God is fully aware of our humanness. He knows how weak we are—creatures of the dust. Compared to his great might, we are utterly weak and vulnerable. And the marvel of this contrast is that God is concerned about our every need. He stoops with compassion to treat us with gentle care. He knows how easily we crumble under pressure.

The apostle Paul had learned how to treat others with gentleness, even though he was naturally a stern, demanding leader. He could remind the Thessalonian believers, for example, that he had been gentle among them, "as a nursing mother tenderly cares for her own children" (1 Thessalonians 2:7). He was in no sense weak in his ministry to people, however—just a few verses later he reminded the Thessalonians, "we were exhorting and encouraging and imploring each one of you as a father would his own children" (2:11).

Such gentle caring is the responsibility of all Christians. Paul issued this very challenge to the Galatian church: "Brethren, even if a man is caught in any trespass, you who are spiritual, restore such a one in a spirit of gentleness, each one looking to yourself, lest you too be tempted" (6:1). Paul wrote this to an entire church, not just to pastors. It suggests that a church should be comprised of people who are sensitive to each other's needs and ready to offer support. Superior attitudes don't belong here, for each is subject to the same temptations. Therefore, Paul writes, we are to "bear one another's burdens, and thus fulfill the law of Christ" (6:2).

¶ Haddon Robinson writes of this need for gentle caring, quoting a political leader who described the brokenness of our time as "Humpty Dumpty people existing in a Humpty Dumpty world." Robinson suggests that the familiar childhood nursery rhyme "stands as a parable of life." It seems that no one in the kingdom could put the broken egg together—yet if the king had been summoned, he could have done the job. But Jesus Christ is the King of kings. He specializes in putting broken people back together—and he uses us. "As a part of Christ's caring community we can help people walk and show them where to walk," Robinson declares. "We must be about His caring business. Humpty Dumpty men and women don't care how much we know unless they know how much we care."[3]

Our church programs may be scriptural, efficiently organized, and studded with volunteers. They are to little avail, however, unless the people we seek to help sense through us the gentle, caring touch of the Savior.

Paul Welter suggests several ways we can show tenderness to those we seek to help:

1. Be friendly.
2. Accept your friend. Become aware of any judging you are doing, and remind yourself that judging others is not your task.
3. Slow down your voice rate if you tend to speak fast.
4. Affirm the other person. Tell him his strengths as you see them. Let him know you're glad to be with him.
5. Work hard to get with the emotion he is feeling.
6. Try smiling with your eyes as well as your mouth.
7. Think about his interests and his needs.[4]

Several of these principles were beautifully demonstrated by one of our workers. Carol, a young married woman, was seeking to help another young woman, Debbie, whose husband was not a Christian. Debbie's husband was from another background and had little time for Christianity. Debbie had become very discouraged and had quit coming to church.

Then Carol entered the scene. She worked at being Debbie's friend, took her to lunch, and invited Debbie and her husband to her home. Debbie began to see that God loved her and could use her testimony. She started coming to church again and to pray for her husband. As a result, Debbie's husband began to comment on his wife's testimony and to ask for her prayers. He even began to come to church with her. He hasn't received Christ yet, but he is still showing interest. Carol has moved to another city, but the results of her caring are still evident.

¶ As we actively seek a sensitive concern for others, we must understand that communication is a vital key. Psychologist Erich Fromm stresses its necessity if love is to exist: "Love is possible only if two persons communicate with each other from the center of their existence."[5] This communication may be in words, by touch, through a smile, or just in physical presence. Sadly, though, we often fail to communicate much that is positive and constructive. Effective communication can take place only when the message or concern in our heart is effectively transmitted to the other person. And we can measure that effectiveness by whether he feels and understands our message. In our training classes, we teach several steps to improving personal communication skills, especially tailored for use in a caring ministry.

The first step is, *Bathe the experience in prayer.* For the Christian, all effective communication has its roots in prayer. This is the reason for Paul's request of the Ephesian believers: ". . . and pray on my behalf, that utterance may be given to me in the opening of my mouth, to make known with boldness the mystery of the gospel" (6:19).

Although Paul was referring to communicating the gospel, the same need exists for communicating love in a caring ministry to fellow believers. For this reason we teach those in our program to make their communication with others a matter of constant prayer. We find that this often keeps us from blundering into what we had hoped would be a caring contact with the finesse of a bull in a china shop. This habit also reminds us to keep going back to prayer for our own encouragement and for the wisdom we need to keep helping others.

We've found that it's dangerous to move in too quickly, perhaps with grandiose ideas of our ability to effect changes in another person. Because of this danger, a second step we teach our people is, _Go slowly!_ In at least one case I had to ask a caring worker to back off. The person he was trying to help appreciated his good intent but was repelled by his aggressiveness. We need to remember that we are dealing with people, and people respond to tenderness.

Find out the real needs, we also tell our workers. Otherwise, we may end up answering questions that haven't even been asked, applying the salve of our loving ministry to areas of people's lives where they do not hurt.

In order to find out where people are hurting, the next step we need to take in our communication with them is, _Be a good listener._ I have had to learn some lessons in this area. Those of us who are involved in ministering to people find it's just too easy to dominate the conversation. Someone has proposed that we subscribe to a "listening contract"— just as a personal reminder to keep in front of us:

I am going to listen to you right now, better than you have ever been listened to in your whole life. I am going to try to make you feel that you are the most understood person in the world. I will not judge, assume, criticize, give advice, or do anything that might keep you from sharing your true feelings. I am going to give you 100 percent of my attention and all the love of which I am capable, strictly and solely to focus on understanding you now.

We'll often learn much more of what the true needs are and how to meet them by listening instead of talking. This kind of commitment to listening will take us a long way in caring for others.

Keep in mind that gossiping about what someone else shares with us of his personal needs and concerns will shut the door faster than anything else. Above all, *Keep confidences.* Growing relationships are developed by building and maintaining personal trust.

Another important step to sensitive communication is, *Don't preach!* We are vehicles of Christ's love, not advice dispensers or amateur counselors. Any attempt to offer advice, especially in the earlier stages of contact, will probably close the door. One young man said of a well-intentioned caring worker, "I simply mentioned an idea I had and he began to tell me all the reasons it was wrong. I just don't respond to that kind of help."

Just as important as checking our impulse to preach is the principle, *Don't judge!* A counseling professor has advised me that among the basics for "gut level" communication is the rule, "no judging and no advice—unless it's specifically asked for." Since gut level sharing is essential to this kind of ministry, we must be careful to listen with an open mind.

Once we ferret out what a person's true needs are by listening carefully with an open mind, we need to communicate to him that we are genuinely concerned about what he's expressed. A sure way to do this is, *Be sympathetic!* "Rejoice with those who rejoice," Paul says, "and weep with those who weep" (Romans 12:15). Paul is describing empathy, or *feeling with* the other person. Sympathy, as we use the word, means *feeling for* another person. The caring person needs both. It is vital that we try to see the problem from the other person's perspective, perhaps by asking ourselves, "If I were he, how would I feel?" We may never have gone through the same experience, but our honest attempts to understand will be appreciated. Gary Collins uses the term *warmth* to describe this kind of sympathetic approach:

> *Warmth* is somewhat synonymous with caring. It is friendliness and consideration shown by facial expression, tone of voice, gestures, posture, eye-contact, and such non-verbal behavior as looking after the helpee's comfort. Warmth says, "I care about you and your well-being."[6]

A crucially important principle for gentleness in our communication is, *Be encouraging!* While we must try to identify with the hurts of others, it is also important that we maintain our own objectivity, in order to help someone else out of the mire of discouragement. Verbal expressions of care and concern may help here. A short prayer with and for the person is also important. Never use that prayer to preach a sermon, however. Make it a sincere plea to God for help, strength, and—if appropriate—healing.

Along with prayer, the most effective encouragement often comes from reading the Scriptures—before or after prayer, depending upon how the Lord leads you. Just reading a short Psalm without comment is often very effective: Psalms 16, 23, 27, 40, 42, 62, and 91 are some good choices. Another possibility is to share a key verse or passage with the simple comment, "This has meant a great deal to me in times of need." Passages such as John 10:27-30, 14:1-3, Philippians 4:6-7, or 1 Peter 5:7 are often effective in lifting the spirits and turning one's attention to God's care for us.

On Your Own

1. Read through Psalm 103 carefully a few times, paying special attention to verses 13 and 14. Based upon David's description, how would you characterize God's care for you?

2. Read through chapter 2 of 1 Thessalonians, in which Paul recounts his ministry within the Thessalonian church. Judging from verses 7 and 8, how did Paul practice the kind of care David speaks of in Psalm 103? Try to answer in terms of specific actions and behavior what Paul may have had in mind.

3. What could you do to practice this kind of caring with someone this week?

PART THREE
Caring
Where It Counts

9
Caring For The Elderly

Grow old along with me!
The best is yet to be,
The last of life, for which the
first was made:
Our times are in His hand
Who saith "A whole I planned,
Youth shows but half; trust God:
see all nor be afraid!"[1]

David Moberg of Marquette University writes of a phenomenon that he calls "the graying of America," noting that one person in nine is over 65—and in some communities, the ratio is one in four.[2] Some 22 million Americans are now in this age group, which represents 15 percent of the population. And yet we are a youth-oriented society. We laud the beauty and vigor of the young, who are the targets of Madison Avenue's advertising campaigns.

This obsession with youth is true not only of the secular world, however, but also of the church—which tends to program its ministries chiefly for youth and young families with children. Because of this tendency, the church is failing to minister to a large segment of the population—and consequently failing to meet the needs of a significant group within its own ranks.

According to Moberg, the church often dishonors the elderly. He insists that although the church is the best-equipped institution in our society to help retired people, many congregations "have yielded to cultural standards that have contributed to the problems of senior citizens." Moberg then cites some of the discriminatory practices that reflect secular attitudes.

- Our emphasis on youth and families with young children.
- Our appointment of younger members to positions of leadership.
- Our scheduling of programs in evening hours when it is difficult for the elderly to get out.
- Our emphasis on outreach (evangelizing) which seems to leave out the elderly.
- Our focus in pastoral care on only those persons with acute needs.[3]

Because of our failure to meet the basic needs of the elderly, they often tend to feel left out and unwanted. This situation may lead further into a growing anger and bitterness toward their families, the church leaders, and younger people in general.

¶ Loneliness is a major factor in the elderly's feelings of neglect. One godly lady I know struggles with feeling rejected because she has not seen her only child for over sixteen years. She knows where he is. She writes to him and prays for him regularly but receives no response. He has indicated not only that he wants nothing to do with her, but that as far as he is concerned, she does not even exist. She often finds herself overcome by tears.

Rejection is overpowering. To the person going through it, the reasons for feeling lonely and useless are quite real—although younger people may try to offer logical arguments against such feelings. One elderly person lamented, "My children just get angry when I say I'm lonely." These responses may be products of guilt from younger people who realize they have neglected their elderly relatives but cannot or will not face the situation squarely.

When Christians who profess to have experienced the love of Christ do not show any outward signs of caring, it is no wonder that older people simply sink deeper into a morass of loneliness, rejection, and even despair. Willard Gaylin uses strong words to describe this consequence of neglect: "When individuals feel sufficiently unwanted and unloved—when they feel abandoned by those whom they love—they slip into the most dangerous and painful of psychological states, a depression."[4]

The situation of the elderly confronts us with two immediate conclusions. First, the need is present with us, and it is a growing problem—especially with the increasing longevity of human life. Second, the church ought to be the first to care. What can we do?

¶ In marked contrast to our human perspective, God indicates that he cares equally for people of all ages:
> Listen to Me . . . You who have been borne by Me from
> birth, and have been carried from the womb; even to
> your old age, I shall be the same, and even to your
> graying years I shall bear you! I have done it, and
> I shall carry you; and I shall bear you, and I shall
> deliver you. (Isaiah 46:3-4)

God cares for the elderly. Scripture says little, if anything, about retirement from earthly employment; it says absolutely nothing about retirement from God's program of care. In fact, God promises an unrelenting watch from the cradle to the grave.

God also tells us that there is honor in old age: "A gray

head is a crown of glory; it is found in the way of righteousness" (Proverbs 16:31) Psalm 92:14 establishes the potential of usefulness in God's program for the person who is ripe in years: the older person who has walked with God "will still yield fruit in old age," he will be "full of sap and very green" Although the body may be old and the eyesight weak, spiritual vigor may be stronger than ever.

In bypassing the elderly, the church is missing out on a significant segment of its resources. The Bible tells us, "Wisdom is with aged men, With long life is understanding" (Job 12:12) It also says, "The glory of young men is their strength; of old men, their experience" (Proverbs 20:29, *The Living Bible*). We need this kind of wisdom and experience on the team. Rather than neglecting the elderly and thus imposing a poor self-image upon them, we ought to be including them in our strategy for reaching the world for Christ. Perhaps the psalmist expresses the concern of many of our older brothers and sisters:

> O God, Thou hast taught me from my youth; And I still declare Thy wondrous deeds. And even when I am old and gray, O God, do not forsake me, until I declare Thy strength to this generation, Thy power to all who are to come. (Psalm 71:17)

¶ In his book entitled *Human Development and Education,* R.J. Havinghurst identifies several areas of need among older adults that call for adjustments on their part: decreasing physical strength and health; retirement and reduced incomes; the death of a life partner; an explicit relationship to their own age group; certain social and civil obligations; establishing some satisfactory living arrangements.[5] The church needs to become involved in helping our seniors to make these adjustments. It is not enough simply to pacify our consciences by pointing them to the Sunday school class for their age group or to the Thursday sewing circle. They must know that they are loved and are vital members of the local body of believers.

Once we identify needs among the elderly, we need to plan specifically to meet them, within the framework of our Scriptural commitments: to fulfill the Great Commission to reach the world for Christ; to equip the saints for the work of the ministry (Ephesians 4:11,12); and to demonstrate love and seek to meet the needs of the suffering and the lonely (James 1:27). To do this we must show older adults that we love them and need them by making a place for them in the ministries of the local church. This kind of involvement will give them a growing sense of self worth, help them feel needed and useful, and provide ways for them to cope with loneliness.

I discovered, quite by accident, how to involve in my preaching ministry a woman who has a great heart for the Lord but is limited physically. We had been able to minister to her in several ways, including bringing my sermon tapes to her each week. On repeated occasions, she would share interesting illustrations she had heard on Christian radio broadcasts. I found that for some time she had been recording such illustrations in a spiral notebook. After expressing my appreciation for what she shared, I asked if she would like to help me. This thought delighted her—and I'm sure there are many older people who would be greatly encouraged if they thought their pastor needed their help in some way. I suggested that she continue to take notes on illustrations used by radio speakers, and also record the name of the person who used each anecdote or helpful quotation. Since then she has faithfully supplied me with these useful windows for my sermons. And she is always thrilled when she hears me use one that she has supplied.

¶ One of the most difficult experiences for the senior citizen is the move into a nursing home. This often occurs at the suggestion of a family physician, because the person can no longer take care of himself. The family often struggles with this move. Ideally, the children will make every effort to bring the aging parent into their own homes. But when all other considerations have been ruled out, or tried and finally found inadequate, a special care facility may be the only choice.[6]

Whatever the reasons, such a move is a frightening experience to older people. They feel they are being removed from the mainstream of life, and see it as the last step preceding death. Retirement may have been traumatic, but at least they were still in a somewhat normal world—in a neighborhood, perhaps with families, with the laughter of children and conversation with people of various ages. They could go to the grocery store, drive their cars. But the nursing home is an abnormal world. They live with friends who are sick, senile, and dying. They have nothing to say about their daily schedules of eating and sleeping. Perhaps worst of all, many of the elderly in such homes are seldom visited. How can we encourage such people?

Richard A. Hubbard, Supervisor of Training for the Mental Health Outreach Program at the University of Notre Dame, has offered some helpful suggestions for ministering to those in a nursing home:

- Use non-verbal communication (touch, hug, hand-holding), along with conversation, because age often robs older adults of the sensory skills that most of us rely upon for communication.
- Speak slowly and carefully, avoiding abstract statements. If you're not understood, try to reword the message before repeating it.
- Try to avoid "the interview": repeating questions about the weather and roommates, which can become strained. Be willing to share personal information about your family or job.

- Allow the conversation to focus on the past, without rehashing past failures. Speak of forgiveness when it is appropriate, both at the human and spiritual level. You can also "use the past in the present tense"—updating and orienting them to changes in areas they have been involved in.
- Understand their sense of betrayal, not only through the loss of mates, friends, and family, but also what may seem the ultimate betrayal—the feeling that they can no longer trust their own bodies. Hubbard writes that "their eyes, memory, legs, or bowels may be betraying them."[7]

Some of these same principles could be used to encourage senior citizens wherever we find them. As with people of any age, the key is to treat them with love and respect. They will quickly detect any attempt to talk down to or manipulate them. One eighty-year-old lady, a relative of mine, caught me in just such a maneuver. We had been told that she was in the early stages of senility, and I was trying to discover how far she had progressed. I began to ask her questions about her past and then moved on, directing my questions more and more toward the present, having learned that people with such problems have more difficulty with the present. She suddenly stopped me in the midst of my questioning and, looking me squarely in the eye, said, "I know what you're doing!" I was caught completely off guard by the keenness of her insight. I had not treated her as an equal, and it caught up with me.

¶ We had made several attempts in our church to develop a caring ministry to senior adults, with varying degrees of success—and failure. The need was there, as well as our desire to meet it, but it took us a while to discover that the right leadership was the key. As is always the case, God knew exactly what we needed. He sent us a semi-retired couple—warm, hospitable people with whom everybody immediately fell in love. To our great delight, they had a strong desire to begin a ministry to senior citizens. In May of 1980, they began what has become a significant caring ministry among retired people. While looking back on the beginnings of this group, the leaders wrote,

> As the months passed by we could feel the Holy Spirit with us. We ceased speaking of our aches and pains and started to talk more about what we learned studying the Bible and about prayers we'd seen answered and about our faith in Jesus Christ.

The ministry caught on in an exciting way. The seniors felt that at last they had something of their own. Others began to attend, even those from around the community. After meeting for a short time on a week-by-week basis they decided to give their group a name: the "J.O.Y. Class" (J.O.Y. stands for Jesus, Others, and You).

One of the initial problems we faced was transportation. Most people did not have cars; some were limited physically, and one lady was blind. The group leaders contacted the community "Senior Wheels" office, a civic program that exists in many towns across the country, and a van now shuffles class members to and from church every Tuesday.

The J.O.Y. class is both a Bible study and a caring fellowship. They sing hymns, pray, and share Scripture together, as well as following a structured Bible study course. Interspersed with their regular weekly gatherings are frequent social outings, such as potlucks, birthday parties, and bus trips. The members also make regular phone calls to prayer partners and actively pray for each other's needs. As they have become challenged by the needs of our young people, they have each chosen a highschooler to pray for. They are not only meeting their own needs but also reaching out to others.

Life is becoming more meaningful for these senior adults because one couple has cared. "If you sow seeds of kindness," it's been said, "you will reap a harvest of love." These folks are finding this to be true. Some of them are discovering the truth of a line from C.E. Cowman: "Some lives, like evening primroses, blossom most beautifully in the evening of life."

On Your Own

1. Based upon Job 12:12, Psalm 92:12-14, and Isaiah 46:3-4, what is God's view of elderly people?

2. Prayerfully select an elderly person to whom you could express love (don't overlook your parents or grandparents). What ideas from this chapter seem most useful to you in caring for this person?

10
Caring for the Lonely

Alone, alone, all, all alone,
Alone on a wide, wide sea!
And never a saint took pity on
My soul in agony.

T hese lines from Samuel Taylor Coleridge's poem "The Rime of the Ancient Mariner" tell the story of many in our day. Loneliness! It seems to persistently hang over people like an ominous cloud, robbing life's zest from both young and old. In *Loneliness Is Not Forever,* James Johnson discusses "the mystery of loneliness":

The big frustration is in trying to understand it. It's like chasing a soap bubble in the breeze. Catching one proves nothing; it is only a smear of chemicals that remains in an amorphous state. Like that soap bubble, loneliness can defy definition.[1]

Loneliness is no respecter of persons. It can hound the lives of young or old, rich or poor. Author Leslie Flynn tells of a man who was riding in a taxicab in New York City's Times Square when a note was handed to him which read, "I'd rather you talk to me than tip me. I'm lonely.—Your driver."[2] All of us have a genuine need to know people who will share our deepest concerns. When we lack such friendship we may slip helplessly into an overwhelming depression. Flynn adds,

"Lonely Voices" is not just the title of a song. Some counselors contend that loneliness is the most widespread illness in America today, and have given it the technical term, *meaningless depersonalization.* Many who are not isolated in space are insulated in spirit.[3]

Johnson also comments on how devastating this problem is. He cites an interview with psychologist Dr. James J. Lynch of the University of Maryland School of Medicine, in which Lynch warned of the connection between loneliness and health:

. . . social isolation, sudden loss of love and chronic loneliness are significant contributors to illness and premature death. Loneliness is not only pushing our culture to the breaking point, it is pushing our physical health to the breaking point. . . . For example, the coronary death rate among widows between 25 and 34 is more than five times that for married women. The death rate for bachelors is 75 percent higher than that for married men, and for divorced men the death rate is more than double. Loneliness—isolation from others—takes a tremendous toll.[4]

It's obvious to most of us that loneliness and being alone are not the same—time alone is a necessary reprieve from the pressures of life, and it can be a time of great productivity. But most lonely people don't see it that way. They feel alone in a crowd, and they also feel lonely and depressed when by themselves. The circumstances don't matter much, because loneliness is emotional—it comes from within.

The lonely sufferer isn't likely to understand his own problem. He may blame others and become angry—even at God. All he knows is that it hurts inside, and he wants relief, which he believes will come through people. Some lonely people will go to great lengths to get the attention they crave. I remember a man in his nineties who was constantly calling his relatives with clever, though sometimes flimsy, excuses to get them to visit him. Once he called the local police in the middle of the night, insisting he needed their help. When they arrived he simply said that he was hungry and was too weak to get out of bed to go to the refrigerator. The police obligingly found the food he asked for and served him his snack in bed. He was content when they left, not because of the snack, but because of the human attention he had received.

¶ God knew from the beginning that man would have this need for caring companionship, as we can tell from his declaration in Genesis 2:18: "It is not good for the man to be alone." Jesus evidently had this in mind when he sent his disciples out two by two.

Though some may boast of "going it alone," it is neither normal nor healthy. Others of us may feel that we are second-class Christians when we struggle with loneliness, until we remember that the greatest of men have fought this battle. Elijah, for example, the great prophet who defeated the 450 prophets of Baal on Mount Carmel (1 Kings 18), sank into depression and loneliness when threatened by Jezebel. While hiding in a cave in Mt. Horeb he cried to God,

> I have been very zealous for the Lord, the God of hosts;
> for the sons of Israel have forsaken Thy covenant,
> torn down Thine altars and killed Thy prophets with
> the sword. And I alone am left, and they seek my life,
> to take it away. (1 Kings 19:10)

Although Elijah failed to recognize it, there were 7,000 others in Israel who were faithful to God—but he was alone and without their encouragement at the time. As he fled from Saul, David was also overcome with loneliness. He felt forsaken by God (Psalm 13:1), oppressed by those who hated him (Psalm 42), and sometimes totally depressed and hopeless (Psalm 69:1-4).

Even Jesus experienced loneliness. If this sounds surprising, recall how he struggled with the burden of becoming sin for us as he prayed alone in the Garden of Gethsemane. He had said to his disciples, "My soul is deeply grieved, to the point of death; remain here and keep watch with Me" (Matthew 26:38). The disciples fell asleep, however, and Jesus was left to struggle alone. As he later hung on the cross, and the full impact of suffering for our sins overcame him, he cried out, "My God, My God, why hast Thou forsaken Me?" (Matthew 27:46).

Paul, the energetic apostle to the Gentiles, had lonely times too. Second Timothy 4 records his loneliness as a prisoner of Nero. Most of his friends had departed when he stood trial the first time, so he appealed to his young friend and co-laborer, Timothy:

> Make every effort to come to me soon; for Demas, having loved this present world, has deserted me and gone to Thessalonica; Crescens has gone to Galatia, Titus to Dalmatia. Only Luke is with me. . . .
>
> At my first defense no one supported me, but all deserted me; may it not be counted against them.
> (2 Timothy 4:9-11 and 4:16)

These men all came to grips with their loneliness, however. Each one was overcome to some extent, as he struggled and appeared to exhaust his human resources. But each one also discovered he could get a foothold on victory by drawing upon divine resources. Elijah heard "a sound of a gentle blowing" (1 Kings 19:12). David reminded himself of the Lord's faithfulness to help: "Why are you in despair, O my soul? And why have you become disturbed within me? Hope in God, for I shall yet praise Him, the help of my countenance, and my God"

(Psalm 42:11). Jesus concluded his prayer in the Garden, "My Father, if this cannot pass away unless I drink it, Thy will be done" (Matthew 26:42).

Paul also saw God as his source of help. Though he told Timothy that no human friend stood with him before Caesar, he was quick to add, "But the Lord stood with me, and strengthened me" (2 Timothy 4:17). And, as though to stress the lesson he had learned in his loneliness, he made this positive affirmation in the very next verse: "The Lord will deliver me from every evil deed, and will bring me safely to His heavenly kingdom; to Him be the glory for ever and ever. Amen."

Notice the common pattern among these biblical giants, including Jesus, in their experience of loneliness. First, they discovered that human resources are not enough to cope with loneliness. Second, they all felt the need for the support of other believers. Third, they found their principal source of strength, and the means of overcoming, in their fellowship with God and in submission to God's sovereign ruling—and overruling—in their lives.

This pattern tells us something important about dealing with loneliness: both the *people factor* as well as the *divine factor* are important, and we must learn to avail ourselves of both; but our ultimate satisfaction comes only in intimate fellowship with God. David had Jonathan, but he drew his strength from his fellowship with God. Paul had Luke, but he was ultimately encouraged by the God who stood with him.

¶ It should be our goal to help bring people to the point where they trust God as the ultimate answer to their loneliness. Caring must not ever be reduced to just a humanistic solution to the problems of people. We must learn to care at the human level, but in the process, we must also bring people to the Well where they can drink their fill! This balance of the human and divine elements was brought to my attention in the life of a woman who lost her husband. We had worked hard to show love to this couple, and they had responded in kind, revealing a great capacity for loving others. We had always stressed with them, however, that contentment arises from a growing fellowship with God. After the husband's death, the woman called me one day to say that the night before she had had "the lonelies" and had lain awake crying. In the midst of her tears she remembered that just a week earlier she had written a list of ten things to do when she felt this way. After practicing several of the items, she crawled back into bed and promptly fell asleep. She shared with me her prescription for what to do when loneliness engulfed her:

1. *Pray*—for God's Holy Spirit to comfort you and fill the empty place in your heart.
2. *Cry*—to wash out your heart and soul.
3. *Do*—something for somebody else.
4. *Pray*—for others. Some of their problems can make yours look mighty small.
5. *Exercise*—go for a walk, garden, mow the lawn, wash the car, clean the house, garage, basement, or attic. Then treat yourself to a long, steamy bath.
6. *Brighten up*—your appearance. If you look better, you'll feel better.
7. *Invite*—someone to lunch or dinner, or take him out to eat.
8. *Pursue*—a hobby. Read your Bible regularly and get into a Bible study group. Do volunteer work.
9. *Count*—your own personal blessings and marvel at how good God has been to you.
10. *Read*—a special promise from the Bible. For me it is Jeremiah 29:11—"'For I know the plans that I have for you,' declares the Lord, 'plans for welfare and not for calamity to give you a future and a hope.'"

There is something here for each of us in coping with loneliness. It reminds us that although we need each other, the ultimate answer to loneliness is to be found in a close and satisfying fellowship with God. When we're lonely, however, it's comforting to know that God uses people to help people.

¶ Perhaps nowhere does loneliness seem more incongruous than in the local church. What may seem to be a warm and fulfilling fellowship to one may be just the opposite to another. Author Juanita Wright has recorded some of these lonely voices: "Sometimes I feel lonelier at church than I do when I'm alone. . . . My loneliest hour every week starts at 11 o'clock on Sunday morning."[5]

While discussing the stirring phrase in Isaiah 40:1, "Comfort, O comfort My people," Gaines Dobbins quotes the great preacher, J. H. Jowett, when he was asked what he would emphasize if he had his life to live over. Jowett answered with noticeable emotion, "I would major on compassion and comfort!"[6] This is a ministry ordinary Christians can have: bringing compassion and comfort to those who are lonely. Here are a few practical suggestions for brightening up the lives of suffering people:

Visit. To the lonely person, nothing is quite as important as a personal visit. It is a very tangible way of saying, "I care about you." I have often seen a face brighten when an elderly or divorced person opens the door. It isn't even necessary to have a reason for calling—just "I was thinking of you, so I stopped by." Sometimes lonely people are so hungry for human companionship they do all the talking. They will tell me about their children, their grandchildren, their jobs, or their hobbies. Then when I leave they'll express with enthusiasm their appreciation for my stopping to talk—when I've said hardly a word!

Telephone. The telephone is a useful instrument for providing immediate access to another person. If we know how to use it, we can make that brief contact a caring one. Our warmth and friendliness can brighten the life of the person on the other end. A consumer pamphlet offers some very helpful advice here: "The safe rule is: treat your telephone 'visitor' as if he or she were present. Make your voice warm and pleasant. Get a 'glad to hear from you' ring into it."[7]

Write a note. A short "thinking of you" note or an appropriate greeting card can also be very meaningful. Lonely people, especially, enjoy receiving mail. An encouraging note can be an effective, uplifting antidote, but it should not be preachy or overly emotional. It might be a birthday or anniversary card, a thank-you note for a job well done, or just a message saying, "I prayed for you this morning."

Invite. Lonely people have a persistent longing to interact with others. Many people would recommend that we should invite them to church, and this is a good suggestion. It is far more meaningful, however, to *bring* them to church, sit with them, introduce them to friends, include them in your conversations, and invite them home to dinner. An invitation alone, however well-meaning, may seem like only a courteous gesture to the lonely person. We are often totally unaware of the fears that grip such a person, such as the awesome one of walking into a room full of people, all engaged in what seem to be happy conversations.

I was reminded of this when a divorced woman told me that she felt very uncomfortable and unwanted when she came to church. She testified to a growing faith in Jesus Christ, yet she had a strong sense of being an oddity in a society geared to families. Such people need someone who will care enough to invite them into his or her circle of friends and make them feel loved and wanted.

In sharing her experience of divorce, Amy Ross Young emphasizes the importance of "a group of good friends. The number is not important, but the right mix is. Mine include other singles, some delightful young couples, some older people I have known since childhood—and many couples in my own age bracket."[8]

We can help a lonely person find a group of good friends, and we should also pray about and strive to achieve the right mix to meet the needs of that person.

An anonymous author has summed up the significance of caring for the lonely in this thought-provoking line: "You can measure your likeness to Christ by your sensitivity to the loneliness of others."

On Your Own

1. Read about the remarkable encounter in 1 Kings 19:9-18. How did God enable Elijah to overcome his loneliness?

2. According to 2 Timothy 4:9-18, what made Paul feel lonely, and how did he overcome it?

3. Are you inclined to have periods of loneliness? Review the list in this chapter of ten things to do when loneliness is overwhelming, and then draw up your own list. Be sure to select a key verse to memorize, so you can meditate on it at such times. Keep this list where you can easily turn to it.

4. Prayerfully decide *when* and *how* you will help someone whom you know to be lonely, perhaps by selecting one of the four practical suggestions in this chapter as a means of expressing your care.

11
Caring for the Sick

O ur society is obsessed with good health. We not only desire it, but we seem to demand it. When illness strikes, we immediately ask, "Why me?" We might feel that we are at the mercy of the capricious turns of some roulette wheel. Or we fear that we are being punished for some past wrong. We are afraid of suffering, and we feel that life was never intended to be this way.

British theologian J. I. Packer approaches this issue in an interesting and helpful article intriguingly titled: "Poor Health May Be the Best Remedy":

But today, dazzled by the marvels of modern medicine, the western world dreams of abolishing ill health entirely, here and now. We have grown health conscious in a way that is in itself rather sick, and certainly has no precedent—not even in ancient Sparta.

Why do we diet and jog and do all the other health-raising and health-sustaining things so passionately? Why are we so absorbed in pursuing bodily health? We are chasing a dream, the dream of never having to be ill. We are coming to regard a pain-free existence as one of man's natural rights.[1]

¶ Are we in fact "chasing a dream"? This question presents special problems for the Christian. The person who sees himself living in a world of chance struggles less with intellectual acceptance of the unexpected turns in life, however painful they may still be. But the Christian believes in an orderly universe under the control of a loving God. How does he handle the unsettling experiences that seem to contradict his understanding of this loving God? Some settle the question by declaring that healing is the inalienable right of every true Christian, as part of the atonement package. All that one need do is have the faith to believe. The corollary to this is that if we are not healed, we just lack faith. Dr. Packer responds strongly to this view:

It is here that I gently but firmly demur. This reasoning is wrong—cruelly and destructively wrong—as anyone who has sought miraculous healing on this basis and failed to find it, or who has been called on to pick up the pieces in the lives of others who have had such an experience, knows all too well. To be told that longed-for healing was denied you because of some defect in your faith when you had labored and strained every way you knew to devote yourself to God and to "believe for blessing," is to be pitchforked into distress, despair, and a sense of abandonment by God.[2]

Charles Farah Jr., a writer who comes from a background in which healing has been a major article of faith, seems to agree with Packer. He cites the tragic experience of a couple who, believing God would heal their diabetic son, stopped giving him the prescribed insulin dosage. Three days later their son died. After struggling with this problem, Farah concludes, "There is a difference between faith and presumption." He then goes on to comment,

> Healing is such a complex business that no one but God really has the answers. . . . It took me many years to mature to the conviction that the God of infinite variety has many different ways of healing, but all are evidences of His providential grace. . . . If God is the Source of all healing and Jesus is our model for today, why can we not accept medical science and healing by prayer as equally provided by our Father's loving care? Why should we send millions of sincere, Spirit-filled Christians on a guilt trip for using medicine when medicine is also part of God's great healing plan?[3]

Yes, this dream-chasing is indeed a guilt trip for many. When the long-sought-for and prayed-for healing doesn't come, a great deal of heart-searching follows. Unanswered questions flood the mind, as well as feelings of having been treated unfairly—"others have been healed; why not me?" Anger then develops, as well as depression. But the inescapable fact is that all are not healed, and there are no easy answers. For reasons only he knows, God chooses not to heal some people. Even the great apostle Paul, whom God had mightily used to heal many others, had to leave his fellow-worker, Trophimus, sick in Miletus (2 Timothy 4:20).

¶ Perhaps the most nagging questions in times of illness are the unanswerable ones. An elderly lady enters the hospital for her twenty-fifth bout with major surgery. She asks me, with a pitiful look in her eye, "Pastor, why?" Sometimes a sick person will ask, "Why me? What have I done?" The disciples asked a similar question when they saw the man who had been blind from birth: "Rabbi, who sinned, this man or his parents, that he should be born blind?" (John 9:2). The answer Jesus gave was not what they were expecting: "It was neither that this man sinned, nor his parents; but it was in order that the works of God might be displayed in him" (9:3). In his sovereignty, God allowed it to happen to accomplish his own purposes.

Albuquerque hospital chaplain Dennis Saylor suggests that our submission to the sovereign purposes of God should lead us to ask a different kind of question: "Perhaps, instead of asking, 'Why me?' a more constructive and productive question might be, 'What, Lord?'"[4]

To ask this latter question, we need to look to the Lord to find out what he wants us to learn in the experience. We must remember that God has not singled us out as a target for his vengeance; rather, we succumb to illness simply because we are human. We are subject to the same bacteria as our non-Christian neighbors.

We do have certain distinct advantages as Christians, however, in facing illness. We know, for instance, that God may choose to protect us because it fits his purpose for us at a particular time—as he did for the nation of Israel during their forty years of wandering in the wilderness. On the other hand, he may allow us to experience illness—such as Paul's "thorn in the flesh" (see 2 Corinthians 12:7-10), which Paul says was to keep him humble. Paul prayed three times for a healing that never came, and God's answer was, "My grace is sufficient for you." (verse 9). The grace God supplies is always commensurate with our ability to endure. Paul learned that God could display his power more effectively in a body that was outwardly weak. Since it brought glory to God, the apostle testified that he would "most gladly" accept whatever God brought into his life.

A woman I know was leading her Sunday school class when

suddenly she felt faint. There was a tightness in her chest, and she fell to the floor a victim of a heart attack. Later, in the intensive care unit of a nearby hospital, she confided that the attack had taken her completely by surprise. But she also told me, "Pastor, I'm ready for whatever the Lord has for me." We can relieve ourselves of a lot of unnecessary struggle by resting in God's sovereign appointment for us, and then learning what he has to teach us through the experience.

¶ The Christian will always find the Scriptures a principal source of help through the various struggles in life. Peter's first epistle is an especially helpful portion to turn to during a time of illness. In this letter the apostle addresses suffering people across the world. Peter views suffering as the normal experience of the believer, and his letter provides several key passages that are most helpful for meditation during illness.

In verses 6 and 7 of the first chapter, Peter tells us that we must be aware that God does allow his children to experience short periods of trial to test their faith:

> In this you greatly rejoice, even though now for a little while, if necessary, you have been distressed by various trials, that the proof of your faith, being more precious than gold which is perishable, even though tested by fire, may be found to result in praise and glory and honor at the revelation of Jesus Christ. . . .

Notice that this trial is said to be "for a little while." The time frame is not as we see it, but as God sees it in the light of eternity. The purpose is that our faith may be strengthened and perfected, just as gold is purified through a heating process. There are times when sickness is just such a test. We have no reason to feel guilty, and to fear that we are being punished for sin.

Another key passage is found in chapter 4, verses 12 and 13:

> Beloved, do not be surprised at the fiery ordeal among

you, which comes upon you for your testing, as though some strange thing were happening to you; but to the degree that you share the sufferings of Christ, keep on rejoicing; so that also at the revelation of His glory, you may rejoice with exultation.

Peter cautions us in this passage not to think of such trials as foreign to our Christian life. Christ suffered on earth, and so will we. We are to accept the painful intruder of sickness. We are even to rejoice, since we identify with Christ in his sufferings, and we look forward to sharing his glory.

The third passage I like to refer to, 1 Peter 5:10, is even more a breath of fresh air: "And after you have suffered for a little while, the God of all grace, who called you to His eternal glory in Christ, will Himself perfect, confirm, strengthen and establish you." Here again Peter says the suffering is temporary. The results, however, are permanent. The Greek here suggests that God will make the sufferer "solid as granite" and will "fill him with strength" (of character), having laid new foundations in his life. Such are the possibilities God offers in a time of sickness. How could we do better than to trust his word and rest in his sovereign care?

¶ Entering a hospital for surgery is always a frightening experience, fraught with uncertainty, confusion, and fear. Hospital chaplain John M. Robertson has captured some of these feelings in a poem entitled, "Admitting Office":

Here I am, God,
  sitting in the Admitting Office
  waiting to be admitted.
Here I am
  feeling so afraid
    and so uncertain
  filling out forms
    giving information

CARING FOR THE SICK   119

getting ready
  to turn over my body
to be examined and probed,
  felt and punched,
  cut and put back together;
to be used for
  thermometers and needles,
  pills and medicine.
Here I am
  feeling worse
  wanting to be better.
Here I am, God!
  Where are you?[5]

Bruce Shelley has identified three basic periods for the surgery patient to cope with: 1) the night before and the early hours of the surgery day; 2) the three days or so after surgery when his life signs are low and he is very likely under pain-killing drugs; and 3) the four or more days of return to mobility and strengthened life signs. The patient needs support and encouragement through all of these periods. Shelley suggests that there are at least three basic moods that correspond to these phases: 1) *fear*, almost always a part of the pre-surgery hours; 2) *aloneness*, common during the first six or seven days; and 3) *depression*, common about the fifth or sixth day because of impatience with recovery rates.[6] It is important to keep these needs in mind when visiting a patient, either in a hospital room or in his home.

Despite its activity, a hospital is a lonely place, and visits can mean a lot. Don't go with high goals of ministering to a captive audience, however, especially when the person is very sick. Be gentle, caring, considerate, and exercise restraint—you'll gain much more ground that way. Following are a few guidelines to consider in caring for a sick person.

1. *Visit before the surgery.* The period before surgery is

a crucial time, and it will mean a great deal to the patient and his family to have some caring support. If you don't feel that you should be there, an evangelical pastor may be the one to call. You could make such a visit the night before, or early in the morning about an hour before the surgery is scheduled. This is a time for reassuring words, a gentle touch, the reading of a Psalm, and a prayer for God's presence and guidance in the operation.

2. *Minister to the family.* I have often taken the patient's family members to coffee or a meal during the seemingly endless wait while their loved one is in surgery. This tells them that I care and also helps them to pass the time. There are other ways to help the family, however: baby-sit to free a mother to visit the hospital; bring food to a family while one member is sick and there is little time for cooking; offer transportation to and from the hospital. All can be gestures of love during times of stress.

3. *Visit after the surgery.* This is important, but don't go too soon, such as on the day of surgery. The patient is often heavily sedated and may not even remember your call. Usually, only the nearest loved one should be present during this time. The same rule often applies to the day after major surgery, when the patient may be experiencing the greatest discomfort.

The second day is often a good day to call (if in doubt, contact the family). There are certain areas of the hospital, however, where you will not be able to visit unless you are a close relative or a pastor: the Intensive Care Unit (I.C.U.), the Coronary Care Unit (C.C.U.) and certain cases in which the patient is in isolation. (If you are not sure, check with the family or at the nurses' station.) Another area with limited access is the Maternity Ward, where only the immediate family is normally allowed to visit. In the more critical cases your best help could be given to the family, who might be spending long hours in the waiting room.

4. *Be discreet!* Generally, visits should be short—about fifteen minutes. Usually only two, or possibly three, people should be in the room at one time. Make every effort to be subdued, not only out of deference to the patient you are visiting but also in consideration of the other patients who might share the room. Don't speak loudly or make jokes and by all means do not sit on the bed!

5. *Be encouraging.* There are certain things you should not discuss in a hospital room or sick room at home. For example, it is not the right time to share your experiences of surgery or those of a friend or relative. Do not probe into the patient's medical condition, because he may feel it is too personal to discuss. Do not give medical advice, and do not discuss how much it's going to cost. (There may be an exception to this if the person is well on his way to recovery, and if you are planning to help with the costs.)

There are positive things you can share, such as a bit of encouraging news from "the outside world." You may also share how you are praying for the patient, and perhaps how some are caring for his family during his hospitalization. Again, a short reading from the Psalms is most reassuring, along with a short time of prayer.

6. *Continue to care.* If the period of hospitalization is long, you might want to visit about twice a week. If no one else is visiting the person, this could be more frequent. Visits could then be a little longer, but most of the above rules still apply. Most patients will appreciate some good reading material during the recovery time, and in many cases they will enjoy having you read to them.

On Your Own

1. In the following verses, or in some Scripture passages of your own choosing, make a list of some helpful truths you

could share with a sick person. 2 Corinthians 12:9-10;
1 Peter 1:6-7, 4:12-13, and 5:10.

2. Do a little research on your own, and select some
   literature you should have on hand to share with people
   who are sick. One attractive and helpful booklet for the
   hospitalized is John M. Robertson's *Here I Am, God;
   Where Are You?* (Tyndale, 1976).

12
Caring for the Grieving

No one ever told me that grief felt so like fear."[1] Grief is a universal experience. Every human being is thrust into this grim struggle on one or more occasions during his lifetime. However, the commonness of grief has not made it any easier to understand. Gary Collins comments, "Death and grief are difficult issues to face. When they come we cope as best we can, but otherwise we prefer not to discuss them."[2] Haddon Robinson describes grief as a "wilderness experience": "One of life's wilderness experiences comes when we lose someone we love in death. As certainly as death follows life, so surely we will stumble over that terrain ourselves and we will have to care for others who make that journey."[3]

¶ What is grief? Collins defines it very simply as "an important, normal response to the loss of any significant object or person. . . . Indeed, whenever a part of life is removed there is grief."[4] Usually, we tend to think of grief in connection with death, but we experience it following numerous other losses in life: divorce, retirement, a child leaving home, the loss of a cherished object, to name but a few. Death, however, is probably the most difficult to cope with.

In 1 Corinthians 15, Scripture refers to death as an "enemy" which will one day be conquered. It also describes death as having a "sting," suggesting the pain and suffering we associate with it. It is difficult for us to accept death as part of the life cycle. However, the writer of the letter to the Hebrews makes it clear that death is not only inevitable, but deliberately planned for us: "it is appointed for men to die once" (Hebrews 9:27).

When coping with loss, it is helpful to remember though that our Savior was acquainted with death, and he knew what it was to grieve. Isaiah spoke of him as "a man of sorrows, and acquainted with grief" (53:3). The gospels show him ministering to people who were grieving over death, such as the family of Lazarus in John 11. Here the humanity of Jesus is revealed as he weeps unashamedly at the grave of his friend. Bystanders were so moved by this show of emotion that they exclaimed, "Behold how He loved him!"

Grief is a normal human response to loss. Despite what our society may tell us, it is important for us to grieve. Arthur Freese points out that this experience, or process, is often referred to as "grief work," a term introduced by Sigmund Freud. This description speaks of the task of mourning. It *is* work, and it is painful, slow, and repetitive.[5]

Following a funeral for the death of a spouse, people will often ask me, "Pastor, how is she doing? Is she bearing up?" What they often imply with these questions is that strong Christians ought to endure stoically: although they are hurting inside, they ought to wear a grin-and-bear-it exterior. People tend to think that this behavior is a sign that the surviving spouse is doing well and is going to make it. Nothing could be further from the truth: these apparent signs of strength may actually be danger signals. Hospital chaplain William Miller sounds a needed warning against placing unrealistic expectations on a grieving person:

> The inner voice of inhibition in the griever and the external pressure of "society" to be stoic join and form a conspiracy against the nature of the griever, which is to express authentically the real feelings of the grief experience. And the conspiracy succeeds every time the griever obeys and "pulls herself together." Successfully suppressing the various feelings of grief may win the support of society ("My, didn't she hold up well!"), but the price of the pain of loss must be paid at some time. The human psyche will exact payment with interest.[6]

In his appropriately titled book, *When Going to Pieces Holds You Together,* Miller declares that suppressing the emotions of grief is only asking for trouble later on. To illustrate this point he cites Sylvia Plath's book, *The Bell Jar,* in which the author recalls being overcome by repressed grief over her father's death as she was later visiting her father's grave:

> ". . . my legs folded under me, and I sat down in the sopping grass. I couldn't understand why I was crying so hard. Then I remembered that I had never cried for my father's death. My mother hadn't cried either. She had just smiled and said what a merciful thing it was for him he had died, because if he had lived he would have been crippled for life . . . he would rather have died than had that happen. I laid my face to the smooth face of the marble and howled my loss into the cold rain."[7]

The initial symptom of grief is often shock, a healthy means of defense for our systems at a time of sudden stress. Donald Howard, an Australian minister, wisely points out that this symptom is just as natural for Christians as it is for non-Christians: "the bereaved may act as though nothing had happened. The 'radiance' of some at a funeral may be symptomatic of shock rather than of Christian faith."[8]

Once the shock wears off, other symptoms of grief emerge, often demanding expression when we least expect it. It would be quite unnatural if it were otherwise. One widow said to me months after her husband's death, "I find myself crying a little almost every day." Expressions of grief may be varied, confusing, or misunderstood, but they must be let out. As William Miller says, "it is my observation that 'going to pieces' is the very thing that will hold the griever together as a whole and integrated person."[9]

¶ In 1969, psychiatrist Elisabeth Kubler-Ross published her book, *On Death and Dying,*[10] in which she outlined what she believes to be the stages one passes through in the process of grieving. Although not everyone agrees on the number of stages, or that the process of grief always occurs in such well-defined steps, some exposure to such a progression can help us to understand grief and be better prepared to minister to others.[11]

In his excellent book on pastoral care, Wayne Oates offers a helpful chart showing five stages of grief work. He lists these five steps as a normal "Patient Reaction" after learning of a terminal illness. He then shows five corresponding steps of involvement for the family, the doctors, and the pastor. Each set of steps plays an important role, but Oates' outline of the patient's reaction is especially helpful in understanding what another person goes through in the grief process:

1. *Denial.* Disbelief, isolation; the decision to share or not share feelings about the coming death.
2. *Anger.* Finding adequate targets for anger (for example: doctor, family members, pastor, even God).

3. *Bargaining.* Review of past infidelities to man
   and God. Reversion to the image of self as a "lucky" or
   "unlucky" person.
4. *Despair.* Depression. Mourning over the loss of body
   parts, changes in appearance, disability. Despair over
   excessive medical costs, loss of job.
5. *Acceptance.* Extending the amount of sleep—
   exactly the reverse of decreasing it, as with a child.
   "A final rest before a long journey." "I have fought
   all I can."[12]

Although Oates offers these as the grieving steps for a
dying person, the survivors of that death will have similar
grief experiences. Remember, however, that some people may
experience only part of this progression, and perhaps in a
different order. Also, some phases may be repeated with no
apparent rhyme or reason, as C.S. Lewis describes of his
experience following the loss of his wife:

Tonight all the hells of young grief have opened again,
the mad words, the bitter resentment, the fluttering
stomach, the nightmare unreality, the wallowed-in tears.
For in grief nothing "stays put." One keeps on emerging
from a phase, but it always recurs. Round and round.
Everything repeats. Am I going in circles, or dare I hope
I am on a spiral? But if a spiral, am I going up or down it?[13]

It is painfully obvious that the loss of a loved one is not
easily overcome. The initial shock, mercifully, has a numbing
effect. The real impact of the loss will possibly take months,
perhaps even years. Even then, just when we think we've been
through it all, it may return, just as C.S. Lewis describes it.
Grief has been referred to as "uncharted territory." We grope
our way through what may seem an interminable, and perhaps
endless, maze of emotions. Lewis paints a picture of grief as
"a long valley, a winding valley where any bend may reveal
a totally new landscape."[14]

The struggle seems endless, but God in his goodness does bring healing, stabilizing the mourner once again. One young mother commented, several years after losing her five-year-old son, "You can't get to the happy memories until you work through the sad." The grieving one will usually emerge from the emotional struggle strengthened and able to cherish the happy times which memory has gleaned from the past. Meanwhile, our task as caring Christians is to gently support such a sufferer as he struggles along that uncertain path.

¶ Most of us are more comfortable caring for the lonely, sick, elderly, or even divorced, than for the bereaved. We tend to feel uneasy about how to help a grieving person. A widowed woman who had received a great deal of encouragement and support from another lady in the church summed up such help, however, when she smiled and said with obvious appreciation, "She's always there when I need her." Caring for the bereaved is not so much a matter of words or deeds as it is a quiet, gentle support—offering ourselves as someone to lean on, someone to listen, someone to wait patiently, without comment, while the tears are dried and the story of "how he died" is told again and again. Someone to listen to an oft-repeated recounting of "what a great guy he was."

In the earlier stages of shock and denial, the "just being there" therapy is most important. Haddon Robinson has written an excellent booklet, simply entitled, *Grief,* which is a very useful tool in ministering to others. In it he shares the important ministry friends can have in the early "Crisis Stage":

> Above all they should be there. People want friends
> during grief, and comfort comes when the bereaved
> knows that he is not alone. When a need arises, take
> care of it. Baby-sitting, phone calls, food, laundry,
> errands, transportation, and scores of other details of life
> may easily be overlooked unless a friend steps in.

Robinson identifies the next stage as the "Crucible Stage," a period of more intense suffering that may last three months or longer. This is when many emotional ties with the past must be dealt with and severed. Robinson compares these ties to the ropes that bound Jonathan Swift's fictional traveler, Gulliver: "As in *Gulliver's Travels*, where Gulliver is tied to the earth by the stakes and ropes of the Lilliputians, so the grief sufferer, too, is bound by a thousand emotional cords to the person who has been lost." In this period our physical presence is also important, as Robinson points out: "The late afternoon seems particularly difficult and so are evenings."[15] We could extend an invitation to share a meal, go for a ride, or visit a shopping center. Above all, it is important to listen without attempting to comment. Our part is to listen sympathetically to whatever feelings the bereaved person expresses—even to anger. It also may prove helpful to offer some reading material.[16]

The final stage in the progression of grief is what Wayne Oates calls "Acceptance" and Haddon Robinson calls the "Construction Stage." This is the time when the grieving person begins to emerge from his depression and rebuild his life on new foundations. Robinson urges, "People need to be encouraged to move out into activities as soon as they have the emotional energy to invest in them."[17] Here we can offer encouragement and even practical support, by helping the person to get back into an active life, renewing activities and relationships he once enjoyed. Robinson suggests,

Some people at this time get employment. While volunteer activity may be available, a job where the grief sufferer feels a stronger responsibility to the employer may be even more helpful. Even if men and women may not have to work to earn a living, they may work as a sustainer of life. Others have enrolled in college as a means of establishing new, creative patterns for living.[18]

¶ All of us will suffer grief, but we need not be devastated by it. Those who have learned to walk in fellowship with Christ will be better prepared. David shared his source of strength when he said so beautifully, "Even though I walk through the valley of the shadow of death, I will fear no evil; for Thou art with me; Thy rod and Thy staff, they comfort me" (Psalm 23:4). These reassuring words come from a man who had learned from experience to recognize the protection and security of the ever-present Shepherd. This kind of comfort is the result of carefully guarding our companionship with Jesus and learning to focus our lives upon him. As Robinson declares, "Grief is lessened when we have an eternal center to our lives."[19]

Matthew Henry, the great eighteenth century Bible commentator, offered an encouraging testimony as he anticipated his own death. Because he did not want his friends and loved ones to grieve unduly, he wrote the following message to be read after he was gone:

Would you like to know where I am? I am at home
in my Father's house, in the mansions prepared for me
here. I am where I want to be—no longer on the stormy
sea, but in God's safe, quiet harbor. My sowing
time is done and I am reaping; my joy is as the joy of
harvest. Would you like to know how it is with me? I
am made perfect in holiness. Grace is swallowed up in
glory. Would you like to know what I am doing? I see
God, not as through a glass darkly, but face to face.
I am engaged in the sweet enjoyment of my precious
Redeemer. I am singing hallelujahs to Him who sits upon
the throne, and am constantly praising Him. Would you
know what blessed company I keep? It is better than
the best on earth. Here are the holy angels and
the spirits of just men made perfect. . . . I am with many
of my old acquaintances with whom I worked and prayed,

and who have come here before me. Lastly, would you know how long this will continue? It is a dawn that never fades! After millions and millions of ages, it will be as fresh as it is now. Therefore, weep not for me!

On Your Own

1. In John 11:17-36, read about how Jesus ministered to Mary and Martha as they grieved for their dead brother. Think carefully about as many aspects of Jesus' behavior as you can observe in this passage. What can you learn from him about caring for the bereaved?

2. Identify some Scripture passages that you feel are especially comforting in a time of grief. Which ones would you like to share with a bereaved person? What could you share with him about God as he is revealed in these passages?

3. Select some literature to have on hand to help a grieving person (you might want to take a look at the works cited in this chapter), making sure you familiarize yourself with it before giving it away.

13
A Life of Love

I was armed against argument, ready for rhetoric, loaded for logic. But I had no defense against love."[1]

Caring for people is not limited just to the special cases we have considered. Rather, love is the universal rule of success in all of our dealings with people. Howard Hendricks asks this challenging question: "Has it ever occurred to you that love is the greatest positive force in existence?"[2] Yes, love is powerful. It is effective. It is irresistible.

This primacy of love comes to light in Paul's first Corinthian letter. In chapter 12, he outlines that amazing array of special gifts available to the body of Christ. Yet with all of that astonishing provision for success he is not satisfied; the Holy Spirit compels him to end the chapter by offering something even better. He concludes, "But earnestly desire the greater gifts," and then adds, "And I show you a still more excellent way." With that introduction, Paul launches into chapter thirteen and the greatest description of love in all of literature. Here he teaches us that love is the essential quality needed in all human relationships, and for all of life. It seems fair to say that the Christian life is to be a life of caring.

Paul declares in the first three verses of 1 Corinthians 13 that love is preeminent. As Christians, our dealings with people can succeed only if love is in control. We may claim language ability, the gift of preaching, a thorough grasp of the Scriptures, great faith, and even a willingness to sacrifice all that we have, but it is all to no avail unless God's love is the controlling rule of our life. British writer Graham Scroggie, sums up each of these first three verses in three brief statements: "1) Love should be in possession of our entire emotional nature; 2) Love should be in control of our intellectual powers; 3) Love should dominate the faculty of the will."[3]

In verses 4-7, Paul describes divine love in practical terms. This is the life of caring. The qualities described here are convincing. Manifested in our relationships, they make our Christian life believable. They count wherever we are—in family life or business, in ministry to the lost or the saved, in caring for the divorced or the dying.

The summary statement in verse 8 is a powerful commentary on such a life: "Love never fails." The Christian life is to be dominated by God's love, which is not self-seeking, but sacrificial. The life of the caring Christian should be an unobstructed channel for the free flow of that love to others. To commit ourselves to a life of caring is to be constantly available to the Holy Spirit for effective service until we are called home to Glory.

¶ There is no doubt about God's motives for evangelism. The Scriptures are plain: it was not mere duty or divine urgency that brought the Savior to earth to die on the cross, but love. This supreme motive is revealed in John 3:16—"For God so loved the world, that He gave His only begotten son. . . ." This is one of the most beautiful and best-known expressions of God's love for a lost and dying world. But we are further moved when we discover that God loved us even though we had rejected him. Paul declares in Romans 5:6-8 that few men would give their life to save a good person, yet Christ died for those whose lives were in no way pleasing to him: "But God demonstrates His own love toward us, in that while we were yet sinners, Christ died for us." This is our model for loving the unlovely as we seek to win them to Christ.

When God's love prevails in our lives, it becomes our most effective tool in attracting the lost to Christ. Some call this "pre-evangelism"—the process of getting people's attention so that we can verbally declare the message of deliverance which we call "the gospel." Howard Hendricks uses a quaint yet effective illustration from fairy-tale lore to challenge us to this responsibility:

> Do you remember the fairy tale of the ugly toad who was really a handsome prince? All he needed to break the spell of the wicked witch was a kiss from a beautiful maiden. But what beautiful maiden would stop to kiss an ugly toad? Obviously, only one who stopped first to talk to him and get to know him.
>
> We who wear the beauty of Jesus Christ through His grace pass by many frightened, lost, ugly souls.
>
> A hurried, superficial touch of courtesy cannot convey a message of love. It can only begin. Love moves into the realm of need, flows into a life to share remedies.[4]

¶ In the Great Commission in Matthew 28:19-20, Jesus calls upon us to "make disciples," to baptize them, and then to "teach them to observe all that I command you." The first step in making disciples is evangelism and the second is follow-up. In *Disciples Are Made—Not Born,* Walter Henrichsen summarizes this care of the new convert in the brief statement, "Follow-up, then, is nothing more and nothing less than parental concern coupled with common sense."[5]

Every parent knows that caring for an infant involves more than the mechanics of bottles and diapers. The constant, reassuring love of mom and dad is critical to his development. Henrichsen insists that this kind of environment is essential in the healthy growth of the new believer in Christ: "One of the basic needs in life is to be loved and wanted. We need to apply the principle of TLC (Tender Loving Care) to our babes in Christ. Envelop the young Christian with love!" Henrichsen then suggests three things we can do to help the young Christian feel accepted and loved: 1) invite him home for meals and make him feel a part of the family; 2) involve him in the warmth and fellowship of the church; and 3) take him along—travel together, play sports together, do things together.[6]

Without genuine love, our spiritual parenting will be mechanical, legalistic, and probably ineffective. Although it may sometimes be possible to urge others to go to church, study the Bible, even witness, without the warmth of love, this will tend to produce robot-like Christians who lack the sensitivities and the graces that make the Christian life attractive. A child who has been nurtured in love is apt to be a loving child and to become a loving adult. This principle is also true in the Christian life.

Paul enthusiastically recommended Timothy to the Philippian church as a discipler who would really care about them: "But I hope in the Lord Jesus to send Timothy to you shortly. . . . For I have no one else of kindred spirit who will genuinely be concerned for your welfare" (Philippians 2:19-20). Paul went on to say in verse 21 that many people did not have this concern for young believers, but instead were self-centered. He was confident in sending Timothy, however, because he had trained Timothy personally, and the Philippians knew that this younger servant of Christ was trustworthy: "But you know of his proven worth that he served with me in the furtherance of the gospel like a child serving his father" (verse 22). Timothy had learned to give loving care to younger believers because that is how Paul, his father in the faith, had trained him. And a loving child is likely not only to become a loving adult, but also to produce another generation of loving children.

¶ Augustine taught that the nature of love is seen in the desire of the lover to be one with his beloved. This is portrayed most beautifully on the earthly scene in a happy marriage. The scriptural concept of two becoming one (Genesis 2:24) is the ultimate expression of unity in marriage. It describes the perfect, exhilarating bond of closeness God intends a man and a woman to know when they come together in holy matrimony.

"A successful marriage requires falling in love many times," it's been said, "but always with the same person!" The story is told of one mother whose youngest son asked, "What do people say when they get married, Mother?" She answered rather uncertainly, "Oh, they promise to love and be kind to each other." After some thought, the youngster said naively, "You're not always married, are you, Mother?" The discernment of children is sometimes startling. Jim Groen, president of Youth for Christ International, tells of counseling a teenaged girl who said, "Mom and Dad act like they hate each other. Every night they hassle. They tear each other apart. It's tearing me up too. You wouldn't believe the climate in our house. Sometimes I feel like I'm going to explode and run away." J. Allen Peterson quotes Philip Gilliam, a former Denver juvenile court judge on this problem: "The lack of affection between father and mother is the greatest cause of juvenile delinquency I know," said Gilliam. "It's not how you treat your children; it's how you treat each other, because a child gets his security from knowing that his father loves his mother."

Love in marriage, as in anywhere else, is not just saying so, it is also doing so. I remember a cartoon in which a young couple are embracing each other, and obviously enjoying it. But they are not the only ones carried away by the rapturous moment: their small son dances excitedly at their feet, crying out, "My turn next!" Yes, the love of mom and dad is infectious, and the younger generation picks it up very quickly.

Unfortunately, marriage becomes routine for some people. The little courtesies of courtship days and early marriage somehow get lost in a maze of busyness. Strangely, it is often easier to help people outside the family circle—to visit a friend in the hospital, to change a tire for the widow next door—than to perform small acts of care for those nearest us. It's important that we take time for our family members—perhaps to fix a leaky faucet, to serve breakfast in bed, or to bake a favorite pie.

Children will catch on to the idea of caring, and perhaps even surprise their parents. I'll never forget early one Christmas morning when our three, who were all under sixth grade at the time, turned the tables on us. The light suddenly went on in our bedroom, and three gleeful faces appeared to our half-focused eyes. Our children were singing a Christmas carol and carrying a pot of coffee, two cups, and a Bible. After some laughing and hugs they read the Christmas story from Luke 2 while we leaned back and sipped hot coffee. They were caring! They were telling us how much they loved us, and they are now grown and doing the same in their families.

¶ Ideally, caring begins at home—in a Christian home. It is modeled and then caught by the next generation as a natural part of life, not something that is forced or demanded. As we move through life, it then becomes a natural pattern to express love to those we come into contact with—friends, schoolmates, co-workers. Practical caring also issues freely from a life well taught in the Scriptures—both at home and in the church. With such a background, love is bound to thrive and grow. And people growing in love will spontaneously reach out to those around them: "By this all men will know that you are My disciples, if you have love for one another" (John 13:35).

On Your Own

1. Set some caring goals for your life in the areas mentioned in this chapter: evangelism, discipling, relationships with a spouse, parents, or children.

2. What steps could you take now to start putting these goals into practice and making a real difference in someone's life through the power of love?

Appendix
How to Start a Caring
Ministry in Your Church

The following suggestions are based upon what we have tried and found to work in our caring ministry at First Baptist. Remember that identifying and meeting needs is crucial to the success of a caring program, so be sure to decide carefully about what will work best in your area of ministry as you consider adapting the material on the following pages.

Identifying needs
● Pray with your lay leaders and staff over the needs for caring in your church or area.
● After prayerful consideration, and to the best of your knowledge at this point, carefully outline those needs as clearly as you can.
● Establish goals. First set long-range objectives that you hope to accomplish, giving yourselves a challenging mark to

shoot for. Then set immediate, measurable goals (such as what you hope to accomplish in the period of one month, six months, and so forth) to give you a practical and realistic strategy for achieving your long-range goals.

● Select a leader, or a leader backed by a small committee, to head up the program.

● Decide on a starting date to begin training people as caring ministers.

Select and assemble any materials you plan to use in the program. For example, you could use this book, or a publication such as *Circles of Care Manual,* on caring through Sunday school structures (available for $2 postage and handling from El Camino Baptist Church, 7777 E. Speedway Blvd., Tucson, AZ 85710).

Starting a training unit

Selecting the right people. It is best to choose those who seem to have the disposition as well as the desire to care. Our groups have been a mixture of older and younger adults.

Group size. Make sure each group is small enough to facilitate effective prayer, discussion, and reporting. We have limited our groups to a range of 8-12 people. We've tried larger groups, but they haven't worked out well.

Time involved. Structuring the training around the Sunday school quarter (thirteen one-hour classes) has worked very well for us. This book is structured to be of use with that model.

Class plan. In order to find out what your people already know and what they need to learn about caring for others, you may wish to use a "Pre-Test," an evaluation form that can be given during the first session. On pages 144-145 is a sample of a Pre-Test we've used, along with the answers supplied by one of our groups.

Be sure to begin each class with a time of prayer, for both

the class itself as well as the people for whom you'll be caring.

At the first session, together as a class, make up a list of people in your church who especially need care. Then let each class member select one person whom he or she will care for during the thirteen-week training period.

Set aside a time during each class session for the members to report on their caring assignments for the previous week. These reports should be given orally, but you may also wish to use a written report. We have found it helpful to use a "Caring Evaluation" sheet at the halfway point in our training program. See page 146 for a sample of such a form (also containing the answers from one of our caring groups).

Include a time of teaching during each session. You may want to use the thirteen chapters of this book as your curriculum, or just the "On Your Own" sections at the end of each chapter as assignments. You also might find it helpful to use study handouts, similar to the sample on page 147. I suggest you make up your own, drawing on the material and the Scriptures in the chapters of this book. You could either distribute the handouts at each session for note-taking, or assign them to be completed by the next class session.

Concluding the training unit

In order to evaluate the effectiveness of your training unit and determine how each person may fit into your caring ministry, you may find it helpful to use a final evaluation form at the close of the thirteen-week training period. On pages 148-149 is a sample of the evaluation form we used with one of our groups.

In addition to conducting an evaluation at the end of the training period, we also provide each class member with an opportunity to make a commitment to a caring ministry. The sample form on pages 150-151 offers five possibilities for involvement, and we are currently extending this to seven areas:

- caring by shepherding (assisting the deacons in their shepherding program)
- caring by hospitality
- caring by participating in the church prayer chain
- caring by greeting, following regular church services
- caring by physical help (transportation, meals, and so forth)
- caring by encouragement (showing friendship)
- caring by sponsorship (befriending and helping new converts and new members).

On page 143 is a flow chart for our caring model, which outlines the general progression of our program.

Flow Chart for the Caring Model

A small group of from eight to twelve people is recruited from the congregation for each cycle of the training unit. The group receives thirteen weeks of training (one Sunday school quarter) in providing pastoral care at the lay level. Upon completion of the training, and taking into consideration individual preference, each person is placed in a continuing program in which he can exercise his caring skills.

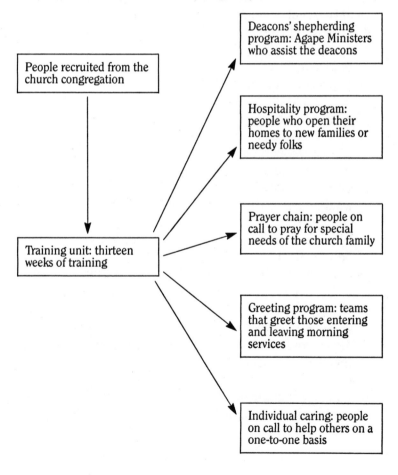

SAMPLE FORM: PRE-TEST

This evaluation is given at the beginning of the training unit. The answers are from a class of ten people.

1. Do you like yourself? Yes __(9)__   No __(0)__
   Unsure __(1)__

2. Can you love another person if the love of God is not real to you? Yes __(2)__   No __(8)__

3. If you are selective in showing love to people, is the love of God real to you? Yes __(2)__   No __(8)__

4. Love requires that you (check three best answers):
   a. say so. __(5)__
   b. give material gifts. __(0)__
   c. give of your time. __(7)__
   d. listen to the person loved. __(10)__
   e. give advice. __(0)__
   f. rebuke the person. __(0)__
   g. visit frequently. __(0)__
   h. give up personal desires to help. __(8)__

5. Can you honestly love someone and refuse to give him what he needs (if you have it to give)? Yes __(1)__
   No __(9)__

6. When a church member is in need or lonely (check the best answer):
   a. the pastor should be the one to meet the need. __(0)__
   b. the person's family should be asked to meet the need. __(0)__
   c. whoever is nearest them should meet the need. __(10)__

7. Most people who have problems have brought them upon themselves. True __(2)__   False __(4)__ (Four equivocated in their answers.)

8. Can a person give love if he has never received love from another human being? Yes __(1)__   No __(9)__

9. People are lonely because someone has failed to show love. True ___(9)___ False ___(0)___ (1 was uncertain)
10. If you should visit a recently bereaved person would you (check the best answers):
    a. tell him God loves him? ___(6)___
    b. listen to his story? ___(9)___
    c. tell him not to cry? ___(0)___
    d. read to him from the Bible? ___(9)___
    e. pray with him? ___(10)___
    f. give him something to read? ___(2)___
    g. give advice on how to get over his grief? ___(0)___
    h. talk about the departed loved one? ___(2)___

Your Name _____

What would you like to get from this class?
   Be able to better counsel those in need. (6)
   Be able to show God's love to those in need. (3)
   Be able to pray effectively for those in need. (1)
   Know when to help and when to say no. (1)
   Be aware of the needs around me. (1)

SAMPLE FORM: CARING EVALUATION

We used this evaluation at the midpoint of our training unit.

Your Name _____ Date _____

Person being shown care _____

Address of this person _____

What did you actually do to express care? Check the following and comment as appropriate.

1. I observed their need, which was (loneliness, someone to listen, someone to show love, encouragement, etc.)

2. I contacted them by phone __(7)__, by writing a note __(0)__, by visiting __(8)__, other (invited to home)

3. I listened (all 10)

4. I encouraged them by (listening, kindness, Scripture, prayer)

5. I read Scripture __(3)__, I prayed (5)

6. I gave material or physical assistance by (taking to doctor, taking to shower, cleaning, helped with shopping)

7. Other notes (use back of sheet if needed): _____

_____

8. Are further contacts needed? (6 said yes)

   If so, for what purpose? (to continue encouragement)

   How often? (occasionally, once a week, every other week)

   Will you do this? (6 said yes)

   Should someone else do this? (2 said yes)

   Who? (pastors)

SAMPLE FORM: STUDY HANDOUT

Caring is Rooted in Love

Jesus taught that love fulfills the law. Every believer is responsible, therefore, to practice the law of love. In the manward direction, this is caring. Consider Matthew 22:35-40.

1. What does the lawyer seem to be looking for in asking this question? (verses 35-36)

2. What is the greatest of all commandments? Why? (verses 37-38)

3. How is the second commandment like the first? Do you see a relationship between these two commandments? (verse 39)

4. How important are these two commandments? (verse 40)

5. What conclusions can you draw from this passage about what Jesus expects of believers today?

Other Notes

SAMPLE FORM: FINAL EVALUATION

This was the final report from the trainees at the end of the training unit. The answers given are compiled from the trainees' responses.

Your Name _____ Date _____

Person(s) you cared for _____

1. I came into the Training Unit because (check all answers that are true for you):

    a. I felt duty-bound to do so. ___(0)___

    b. I sensed needs in my life to be a more caring person with others. ___(7)___

    c. I was concerned about and wanted to do something for people who needed help. ___(8)___

    d. I was concerned that our church should become a caring fellowship. ___(8)___

    e. Other _____.

2. I feel I have a better understanding of what kind of a person a "caring person" is.

    Yes ___(8)___   No ___(0)___   Perhaps ___(2)___

3. I feel I understand better the hurts of people who need caring.

    Yes ___(10)___   No ___(0)___   Perhaps ___(0)___

4. On a scale of 1 to 6, please indicate your comfort level in caring for the following types of people in need (1 = least comfortable; 6 = most comfortable):

	1	2	3	4	5	6
the lonely	1	1	4	4	3	2
the aging	0	2	5	0	5	3
the sick	1	1	0	4	4	0
the dying	3	3	1	1	0	1
the bereaved	0	2	3	3	1	1
the divorced	1	1	2	5	0	1
other	0	0	0	0	0	0

5. As a result of the Training Unit, I have grown in my ability to care in the following areas:

	no improvement	some improvement	much improvement
how to listen		8	3
what to say		7	5
what to do		7	5
when to advise		5	7
literature to give		5	7
Scriptures to use	1	7	3
how to pray	1	7	3

Please comment below on your experience in caring for the one(s) assigned to you during the class:

1. How have you expressed care?
   (by listening, telephoning, providing transportation, helping in the home, etc.)

2. How did the person(s) receive the care you expressed? (most expressed great appreciation; one reserved.)

3. What did this caring experience do for you?
   (deepen understanding of people and their needs; sense of accomplishment; awareness of own inadequacies.)

SAMPLE FORM: COMMITMENT TO A CARING MINISTRY

1. I am now ready to let the Lord use me as he chooses to express care to others in need.

   Yes __(9)__ No __(0)__ Not sure __(2)__

2. I am willing to pay whatever price is required to serve the Lord in this way.

   to give time __(9)__ to give energy __(8)__ to give materially __(8)__ to respond patiently __(8)__ to keep confidences __(10)__

FUTURE INVOLVEMENT

1. I want to be available as a caring Christian in our church in the following ways:

   a. to assist in the deacons' shepherding program as an "agape minister." (4) _____

   b. to assist in the hospitality program by opening my home to people in need. (6) _____

   c. to be a part of the prayer chain. (8) _____

   d. to help in the greeting program. (6) _____

   e. to be on call to care for individuals when the need arises. (7) _____

2. I feel that the Caring Model (check the answers that are true from your viewpoint):

   a. has meet a real need in our church. (10) _____

   b. has met a real need for me. (9) _____

   c. should definitely be continued. (11) _____

   d. needs a great deal more development before it will be useful. (0) _____

   e. should not be continued. (0) _____

Other comments you want to make about the Training Unit, its value, its future, etc.

(Everybody should have the opportunity of taking this training.)

(It seemed to bring people in this class closer together.)

(I think this class is very valuable to the church.)

(Give more helpful handouts, in addition to the ones given.)

Notes

Chapter 1. Does Anybody Really Care?
1. Benjamin B. Warfield, "On the Emotional Life of Our Lord," *Biblical and Theological Studies,* ed. Princeton Seminary faculty (New York: Scribners, 1912), page 42.
2. Warren W. Wiersbe, *Be Real* (Wheaton: Victor Books, 1972), page 138.

Chapter 2. Starting with Love
1. Margery Williams, *The Velveteen Rabbit* (New York: Doubleday, n.d.), pages 16-17.
2. John Powell, *Why Am I Afraid to Love?* (Niles, Ill.: Argus Communications, 1972), pages 23-24.
3. Maurice Wagner, *The Sensation of Being Somebody: Building an Adequate Self-Concept* (Grand Rapids: Zondervan, 1975), page 194.
4. Wagner, page 31.
5. Verna Birkey, *You Are Someone Very Special* (Westwood, N.J.: Fleming H. Revell, 1977), page 3.

Chapter 3. Compassion for the Whole Man

1. Warfield, "On the Emotional Life of Our Lord," pages 40-41.

2. Dean Turner, *Committed to Care* (Old Greenwich, Conn.: Devin-Adair, 1978), page 155.

Chapter 4. The Badge of Discipleship

1. Francis Schaeffer, *The Church at the End of the Twentieth Century* (Downers Grove: InterVarsity, 1970), page 153.

2. Willard Becker, *Love in Action* (Grand Rapids: Zondervan, 1969), page 19.

3. William Barclay, *The Daily Bible Study Series* (Philadelphia: Westminster Press, 1960), page 14:252.

4. Powell, *Why Am I Afraid to Love?*, page 17.

5. Powell, page 17.

Chapter 5. Finding and Healing Hurts

1. Orien Johnson, *Recovery of Ministry: A Guide for the Laity* (Valley Forge: Judson Press, 1972), page 39.

2. Ray C. Stedman, *Body Life* (Glendale, Calif.: Regal Books, 1972), page 25.

3. Stedman, page 25.

4. Stedman, page 51.

5. Schaeffer, *The Church at the End of the Twentieth Century*, page 73.

6. Elton Trueblood, *The Incendiary Fellowship* (New York: Harper & Row, 1967), page 30.

7. Joyce Landorf, *Power,* August 24, 1980.

8. Paul Welter, *How to Help a Friend* (Wheaton: Tyndale, 1978), page 29.

Chapter 6. Becoming a Family

1. Gary Collins, *How to Be a People Helper* (Santa Ana, Calif.: Vision House, 1977), page 131.

2. David Dunston, "The Role of Auxiliary and Supplementary Ministers," *The Churchman,* April-June 1974, Vol. 88, No. 2, page 121.

3. Collins, pages 58-59.

Chapter 7. Learning How to Care

1. As quoted by Arthur A. Rouner Jr. in *How to Love* (Grand Rapids: Baker Book House, 1974), page 106.

2. Arthur A. Rouner Jr., *How to Love,* page 106.

3. Leslie B. Flynn, *You Don't Have to Go It Alone* (Denver: Accent Books, 1981), page 144.

4. Thomas Dubay, *Caring: A Biblical Theology of Community* (Denville, N.J.: Dimension Books, 1973), page 53.

5. Robert H. Schuller, *Your Church Has Possibilities* (Glendale, Calif.: Regal Books, 1974), pages 68-70.

Chapter 8. Adopting a Spirit of Gentleness

1. Anon., "Trouble-Shooting," *Campus Life,* October 8, 1978, page 53.

2. Welter, *How to Help a Friend,* page 211.

3. Haddon Robinson, "On Target," *Focal Point,* July-September 1981, pages 2-3.

4. Welter, pages 214-215.

5. Erich Fromm, *The Art of Loving* (New York: Harper & Row, 1956), page 103.

6. Collins, *How to Be a People Helper,* page 34.

Chapter 9. Caring for the Elderly

1. From the poem, "Rabbi Ben Ezra," by Robert Browning.

2. David O. Moberg, "What the Graying of America Means to the Local Church," *Christianity Today,* November 20, 1981, page 30.

3. Moberg, pages 30-31.

4. Willard Gaylin, *Caring* (New York: Alfred A. Knopf, 1976), page 154.

5. R. J. Havinghurst, *Human Development and Education* (New York: David McKay, 1953), page 2.

6. John Gillies' book, *A Guide to Caring for and Coping with Aging Parents* (Thomas Nelson, 1981), is very helpful for those with elderly parents.

7. Richard A. Hubbard, "Pastoral Care in the Nursing Home," *The Journal of Pastoral Care,* December 1980.

Chapter 10. Caring for the Lonely

1. James Johnson, *Loneliness Is Not Forever* (Chicago: Moody Press, 1979), page 9.

2. Flynn, *You Don't Have to Go It Alone,* page 11.

3. Flynn, page 11.

4. James J. Lynch, as quoted by James Johnson in *Loneliness Is Not Forever,* pages 11-12.

5. Juanita Wright, "Loneliness—No Instant Antidote," *Power for Living,* September 24, 1978, page 8.

6. Gaines S. Dobbins, *A Ministering Church* (Nashville: Broadman Press, 1960), page 176.

7. *What Every Telephone User Should Know,* a pamphlet published by General Telephone System of the Midwest.

8. Amy Ross Young, *By Death or Divorce . . . It Hurts to Lose* (Denver: Accent Books, 1981), page 106.

Chapter 11. Caring for the Sick

1. James I. Packer, "Poor Health May Be the Best Remedy," *Christianity Today,* May 21, 1982, page 14.

2. Packer, page 14.

3. Charles Farah Jr., *From the Pinnacle of the Temple* (Plainfield, N.J.: Logos International, n.d.), pages 3-4 and 13-14.

4. Dennis E. Saylor, *And You Visited Me* (Seattle: Morse Press, 1974), page 16.

5. John M. Robertson, *Here I Am, God; Where Are You?* (Wheaton: Tyndale, 1976), page 4.

6. Bruce Shelley, "How to Make a Hospital Visit," *Focal Point,* July-September 1981, page 9.

Chapter 12. Caring for the Grieving

1. C. S. Lewis, *A Grief Observed* (New York: Seabury Press, 1961), page 7.

2. Collins, *How to Be a People Helper,* page 411.

3. Haddon Robinson, "Good Grief," *Focal Point,* July-September 1981, page 8.

4. Collins, p. 411.

5. Arthur Freese, *Help for Your Grief* (New York: Schocken Books, 1977), page 48.

6. William A. Miller, *When Going to Pieces Holds You Together* (Minneapolis: Augsburg Publishing House, 1976), page 29.

7. As quoted by William A. Miller in *When Going to Pieces Holds You Together,* pages 30-31.

8. Donald Howard, *Christians Grieve Too* (Carlisle, Penn.: The Banner of Truth Trust, 1980), page 13.

9. Miller, page 33.

10. Elisabeth Kubler-Ross, *On Death and Dying* (New York: Macmillan, 1969).

11. If you are a pastor or a Christian leader, you might find the following book helpful: *Death and the Caring Community,* by Larry Richards and Paul Johnson, M.D. (Multnomah, 1980). It contains a fifteen-lesson course on caring for those who are facing death.

12. Wayne E. Oates, *Pastoral Care and Counseling in Grief and Separation* (Philadelphia: Fortress Press, 1977), pages 16-17.

13. Lewis, pages 66-67.

14. Lewis, page 47.

15. Haddon Robinson, *Grief* (Christian Medical Society, rpt. Grand Rapids: Zondervan, 1976), pages 12-13 and 17.

16. Robinson's *Grief* and Lewis' *A Grief Observed,* which I've already mentioned, are excellent selections. Joyce Landorf's *Mourning Song* (Fleming H. Revell, 1971), in which she recounts her struggle with her mother's terminal illness and death, is also helpful.

17. Robinson, *Grief,* page 16.

18. Robinson, *Grief,* page 16.

19. Robinson, *Grief,* page 21.

Chapter 13. A Life of Caring

1. Jim Hancock, as quoted in *Decision*, February 1978, Vol. 19, No. 2, page 15.

2. Howard G. Hendricks, *Say It with Love* (Wheaton: Victor Books, 1975), pages 15-16.

3. W. Graham Scroggie, *The Love Life* (London: Pickering and Inglis, 1935), pages 24, 26, and 28.

4. Hendricks, page 9.

5. Walter A. Henrichsen, *Disciples Are Made—Not Born* (Wheaton: Victor Books, 1974), page 80.

6. Henrichsen, pages 87-88.